One Night

on the Door

Matthew McCourt

Contents

Introduction

"You should write a book; you should write a book!" That's what the new set of doormen I now work with keep telling me and seeing as though the local constabulary have had my doorman badge taken away from me and forced me into semi-early retirement, here it goes. I wish I had kept notes on all the funny stories that have happened on the door, but obviously, being married, I didn't think it was wise but now I'm divorced, I'm gutted I didn't, but there you go; that's life.

Let's get one thing straight before you read any more of my book of stories on the door. I want to make it clear that this is *my* book of stories. I know there will be doormen/ bouncers out there saying they have got funnier stories than me, saying they are harder, stronger, better-looking, funnier, cleverer, richer, than me. No problem; they probably have, but THESE ARE MY STORIES. I do not pretend to be a gangster, plastic gangster, wannabe gangster, I am not and never, ever will be a gangster; I will never be a debt collector, bullyboy, hitman or bank robber. I just worked the door for cash and that's it. Some people might say different, and that is up to them. Let them go ahead and prove it cos if I have not been convicted of it, then it is not true.

In the 22 years I've worked the doors, I have realised that many people see doormen (bouncers) as some kind of gangster crook or doer of evil deeds, because they seem to be the only stories you hear about the people who work in this profession. Never do you hear the stories about how we save people from beatings, drug overdoses etc., etc. The best possible way I could explain a doorman's job is, I would say we are like the police - nobody likes us but everybody needs us at some time. Never do people think that we have interests and professions away from working the door. You know, like we might just be doing the job for extra cash because our daytime job doesn't provide enough money to feed our families and pay our bills.

For me, working the door was not about violence or acting the hard man, it was always about the money. I admit, like in every job, you do encounter pricks working the doors. I have never been naive to this fact and sometimes ended up slapping doormen I have been working with. We have no end of difficult situations to deal with orally, physically and mentally, from old grannies not wishing to pay for a meal because their salad was cold, to listening to some drunkard rabbiting all night that they are not drunk and had no drugs and that they are related to every gangster walking the earth, to some woman wanting to offer you sexual favours just to get in the back door of a venue because the queue at the front door is extremely long.

Working the door has to be one of the best jobs in the world! Every night is different from the last; one night, you can be in a twenty-man stag night brawl, fighting for your life, the next getting paid for doing absolutely nothing.

What I wish to tell you in this book are the funny adventures I have encountered while working at different pubs, clubs, nightclubs, boxing shows, designer clothes sales, and many other venues. All names places and times will be changed to protect the innocent as well as the guilty, but I do hope some people who read these stories do recognise themselves or can relate to some of the situations when they've been pissed.

Nowadays. most books about doormen tell the stories about how hard they are and how many fights they have been in. You will not find any of that Alpha male macho bullshit in here. Hey, I could do that, and trust me, I have been in thousands, and I do mean thousands of fights, got the scars to prove it, both mentally and physically all over my body, from stab wounds to being glassed, but luckily no bullet hole scars. But I wanted to do something different and tell the stories of the funny times I've encountered. I don't want to bore you with stories of stamping on people's heads, head-butts, knuckledusters, baseball bats, stabbings, petrol bombs, arson attacks, shootings, the death threats we receive, and being kicked in the bollocks; we've all read that kind of stories before and they're are all the same.

From a young lad growing up on a tough council estate, I learned how to fight. The only two things the lads learned to do were fight and play football. Mind you, I think heads got kicked just as much as footballs around our way! Oh yeah, there was something else the lads had to learn to do from a young age but they had to have help from the girls to do that, and that came in handy for working the door as well.

I was always dabbling about with boxing and did a bit of judo, but it wasn't until I was 15 that I took up karate with a passion. The style I chose was Wado Ryu, which translated means the way of Peace and Harmony, a rule which I always tried to live by. The karate club I joined was a freestyle sports karate club; it was good but more based towards karate tournaments rather than the traditional side of karate. I didn't care; I loved it! I was hooked. My karate club was affiliated to the NASSKC, and I trained 6 days a week. I trained in my bedroom, I missed school to train, I travelled the country to train, I did seminars, the lot. At the age of 19, I took up boxing as well as still training in karate, but now the karate training was getting down to just a 3-day week, whereas my boxing was a 3-day or 4-day week. On the odd day, I would have a rest. This was usually a Saturday and I would go watch the football for a row; it was in the days of football hooliganism. I know straight away I look like a hypocrite, living the life of Peace and Harmony and then having a tear up on the terraces. So, as you can see, I was pretty well trained and educated in the art of fighting. And as anyone will tell you, once you're trained in the art of unarmed combat, the last thing you want to do is use it, but it is good to know that you can if needs be.

So, at the age of twenty, I became a father for the first time and didn't have a job. I didn't have any money coming in and was on bail looking at a lengthy prison sentence as usual. Trust me, I was innocent; well, I got found not guilty on one of the charges so I guess I was semi-innocent. The police were stitching me up again. You know, they put more stitches into me as a kid than goes into a Royal Princess's wedding dress. Anyway, one Friday night, laid on my mam's couch with no money to even go out, I got a phone call asking if I would like one night on the door working at a club. Well, that one night has turned into twenty-two years of door work! What was funny was that before I started working on the doors, I was never a fan of the doormen. I was always fighting with them. Mind you, I think in the old days the doormen were nearly all aggro nasty bullyboys with a lack of communication skills, I would say. They probably didn't mind having tear ups.

So, that night I took the job and, within a few years, I was head doorman at a bar. I then went on to have a doorman agency for a while, but the SIA badge coming out put an end to that. Some of the lads who worked for me were never going to get an SIA badge, nor were they ever going to pass the police check. This was why I only had decent lads work for me and not the shirt-fillers you see a lot of the times nowadays working on the doors. They are a joke; they don't look like they could deal a pack of cards never mind deal with a fight! Not that I'm judging a book by its cover, I would never do that, but you can just tell a scruffy-looking skinny, greasy-haired spotty-faced young man with a look of no confidence on his face is not going to be able to calm a situation down or deal with somebody to earn their respect, never mind when it comes to being physical. Of course, it's none of my business so I don't care. It's their right to choose that profession and put themselves in that situation.

I have now been retired from working the doors because of some trouble I got mixed up in, not that it matters to me as I was bored of doing it. The police had a helping hand in making sure my badge never got renewed. I never got on with them, never liked them from being a kid. Let them deal with the shit I put up with, week in, week out, but they won't. They'll carry on giving out speeding tickets whilst sat in the warmth of their new Subaru, doing their hair, acting clever, hard and smarmy for some documentary they are filming on SKY. Oh, and for all you do-gooders out there who want to stick your nose in every time there is trouble in a bar or restaurant, etc., etc., you know, the type that go out for a drink once in a while and think they are hardcore, feel the need to join in and become a doorman and stop the trouble but, in fact, they make it worse, here's a message for you. Keep your cocaine-blocked noses out of incidents! You're pissed, you're wired and you talk shit, and the dark and windy nights in Britain last a long, long time. You are worse than the Old Bill and your intervention always ends up making mountains out of molehills, so stick to watching soaps on your big HP television. Trust me, in the long run, it will be safer and cheaper for you.

Here are some of my experiences in those twenty-two years of working on the doors. All these are true; just the names and venues have been changed to protect the innocent, the guilty and the very, very naughty. ENJOY.

1.

Sorry, No Trainers

On the second night of my door career, I was working a venue - let's call it 'WILLY WONKA'S' (not the real name). It was a rough old club which had been shut for years and had now reopened under new management. It was in a very rough part of town near the docks, where the drinkers were hard, the prostitutes were hard, the visiting fishermen were hard, the visiting sailors were hard, the kids were hard, and the dogs roamed around in packs because they were scared of the cats, which, obviously, were hard. So, here I go; straight into a baptism of fire working the door of this rough old club. I remember this club when I was a young boy and my mum's boyfriend would get a taxi there every Sunday because they had strippers on. The good old working-class days, eh? I'm 20 years old now; never thought as a young boy I would be working there. I am stood on the door with a floppy haircut, a bit like that actor, soppy bastard, Hugh Grant, except mine was receding, not a very big frame on me, but still lean because I was still boxing and karate training at the time. The three other doormen working with me at the time, well, two of them were like fucking Frodo and that Dildo Baggins, for fuck sake! I bet they've never been on a rollercoaster in their life, they were that small. Now, don't get me wrong; I never judge a man by his size and when I found out who they were I had heard of their reputations, but when you're about the third or fourth pub along after the docks, some crazy knife-carrying foreign non-English-speaking merchant seaman is not going to give a fuck about the reputation of Jimmy fucking Krankee's twin brothers. The seamen are away on the next tide out so they don't have to worry about repercussions, never to be seen again. The third doorman was alright; a proper gent. He'd done a bit of karate. Years later, it turned out he was a brokeback doorman, not a black belt doorman, but I liked him (not in that way). I liked the way he dealt with situations; always polite and never confrontational. So, here I am; first night on the door at a new club in an old venue that's opened and here are the rules:

1: No trainers

2: No jeans

That's it? You got to be kidding me! We're less than a mile from the docks, in one of the roughest areas of town and that's the rules - no trainers and no jeans? It's a bit like being at a football match and saying to the fans, "Sorry, no scarves allowed."

I couldn't believe it for two reasons: One is it will affect the profits of the club, and the other, it will cause us unnecessary trouble on the door. I mean, let's get it right; at that time, the only people who wore trousers and shoes round there on a night time was the Old Bill and people who stayed out on an all-day drinking session after a funeral. I didn't want to be there when I found out about these rules; I didn't see the point. I always only ever wanted easy money working the doors, and I knew we were going to be busy doing our Gok Wan bit, giving people advice on fashion to go clubbing in this shit hole of a venue. We had a steady flow of people through the door. Then, about an hour after opening, three young lads turned up, very smart, wide boys but not aggro boys, just out on the town giving it large, out on the pull, hair gelled, smart jeans, smart shirts and T-shirts, looking the biz. One of them was wearing trainers, smart trainers, looked brand new like they had been bought that day.

"Sorry, lads, ya can't come in," I had to tell them.

"Why the fuck not?" came the reply.

"Because you're wearing trainers. No trainers allowed, sorry mate; it's the rules." And as I'm saying this, I'm wanting to say to him, "Yeah, it's fucking bollocks, I know. I want to let you in but I can't." So, the lads start doing a bit of huffing and puffing; nothing wrong, talking amongst themselves, just deciding where to go next. With that, three blokes walk up to the door of this venue, probably in their late 40s, early 50s, scruffy as fuck. I mean, these guys were who Frank Gallagher out of Shameless based himself on! They were that scruffy the flies stayed away in case they caught something off them. Their hair was like a 70's Kevin Keegan mullet that had just walked out of a wind tunnel, their trousers were covered in pigeon shit and so were their shirts. These guys had just literally come from a pigeon racing meeting. Their shoes were talking as they walked; know what I mean? The shoes had the soles flapping at the front. You'd have thought they would have put an elastic band around them to stop them flapping about. Then, the head doorman says,

"Alright, gents, in you go, no probs; you're wearing shoes and trousers."

I could not believe what I was hearing or seeing! The three wideboys were looking at me in astonishment. To be honest, if you had walked past you would have thought we were having a 'who can open his mouth the widest' contest, so of course, they chirp up;

"What the fuck is that all about? You're having a fucking laugh, aren't ya?" I had to agree with them, it was a fucking joke, but it was the rules set by the geezer who owned the place, or shall I say, rules set by the guy who fronted ownership of the venue. The three wideboys started to shout insults at us, and I had to agree with their anger. I tried talking to them and got them to calm down, then one of them said to me quietly, "I'm coming back to burn this place down."

I replied, "Mate, if ya thinking that's a way of getting back at them, you're wrong. You'll be doing the owner a favour, but just letting you know I don't think he actually owns it. I think he's fronting it for some dodgy characters you don't want on your case."

I could see him rethinking what he had just said, then he looked at me and said, "Yeah, you're right. I heard rumours who it's owned by; you're alright, you are." They all shook my hand and walked off into the night.

Job done in the way of Peace and Harmony.

That night, somebody tried to burn the place down; a failed arson attempt. I never told anybody what one of the lads had said, as I didn't believe it was any of them. I genuinely thought it was something to do with the people who owned it and if they had heard the rumour about the lads saying that, they would have found out who they were and somehow turned that rumour into the truth by torture or painful reasoning.

I did two more weekends there and then I was gone. I couldn't wait to get out of there, so I moved on to a rave club. I think that place only stayed open a couple of more months then shut down. I never bothered asking or finding out why; my own theory would be that people probably ended up getting pigeon chest or tinnitus from the noise of all those shoes flapping about. What a shit hole! Yeah, I had some fights there - floppy-haired skinny young lad, I looked like easy pickings for the old unfit has-been war horses of that area. Never mind; we live and learn.

2.

Doorman Getting Spiked

I start working this rave club and I loved it. I loved everything about it; loved the music, the vibe, the goings-on, late nights, the girls, the aggro; it was great working there. It was split over two floors; downstairs was the old skool garage music, while upstairs was all the Techno stuff that had just started to be born. Techno did my head in with all the young lads with the whistles and yellow gloves. Sometimes they'd wear them all in white paper suits; you know the ones I mean, like the Old Bill give you when they take your clothes away for forensics. We had all the top DJs there, Carl Cox and the like; we had 2unlimited and The Prodigy turn up; they were a great bunch of lads. We had everybody who was anybody at that time. There were loads more famous names but I can't remember who they were. The fact is, I didn't know who most of them were but I didn't really give a fuck as long as I got paid and got my perks at the end of the night. The drugs were rife in this place; they were all over. Most of our trouble was to do with dealers fighting out to control the market in the club. None of the doormen got involved in taking cuts, bribes or backhanders off the dealers. We were all into positive stuff, boxing, martial arts and all that. The way I think we all looked at it was you sometimes have to train kids and most kids look up to you, so getting involved in anything like that was a no-go. There were six of us on the door; just six! It held 800. Let me put that again

17

- its fire limit was 800. We had clickers on the door so we could keep count of how many we had in, not that it mattered because we just let people in and in and in and in. The night Carl Cox came we had over 1000 people in the place. When Prodigy came, the last count on the clickers was about 1200. You couldn't move! If there was any fighting anywhere in the club, we would never have got to it.

I used to be on the front door, controlling how many we let in at a time to the cash desk, checking ID for underage and doing the drug searches, which, to be honest, was a waste of time. All the dealers did was get the women to bring the drugs in, tucked in their bra or down their knickers. Looking at some of the tarts knocking about with these dealers, I would be surprised if the bag didn't melt being stuck down their knickers. These women were so rough, Jeremy Kyle's minders would not mess with them.

So, as I was saying, it was a buzz just to work there and doing the front door had its perks; you know, let a girl in as your guest and when the club shut, she let you in as her guest. The only thing was when you let a guest in, the people who owned the club looked at it as losing a fiver, yeah right, like a fiver they would declare to the taxman, so their next move was to take me off the front door and put me upstairs amongst all the techno music; all the kids running round in the fucking white suits like the CSI wear, fucking whistles, glowsticks, gloves and all the rest of it. God, I hated techno; still do. So, my dummy is out. I'm sulking, already looking for my next venue to work because there is no way I'm staying here and listening to this shit every night.

So, there I was, partnering an old friend from the estate where I grew up. I'd got my earplugs in, no smile, daydreaming of the sweet mellow soul music waiting for me on my car stereo when I finish this shift. Next thing, my partner, who was called Glen, is up on the speakers going mental. Now, when I say speakers, this was well back in the day when Health and Safety meant don't smoke and look both ways when crossing the road; these speakers were 8ft tall and 5ft wide and proper blasted music out, if you could call it music. There were loads of them placed around the upstairs of this club. I'm thinking to myself, 'What the fuck is that silly bastard doing?' Then he takes off his dicky bow, then his shirt - body like his he should have kept his shirt on, the podgy pink bastard - it was like watching Porky Pig dance and 'that that that that's not all folks'; he spins round and starts shaking his arse! Obviously, I've clicked by now - he's been spiked. I can't believe it. I'm partnering a doorman who loves everybody, who thinks he's a Chippendale, then with that, with his back to the adoring, gurning, whistling, hands-in-the-air crowd, he only tries to do a backflip off the speaker and lands on his head. Fucking great! Now I've got an unconscious doorman on the floor surrounded by 200 or so whistling gurning zombies and there's not a chance in hell am I giving out the kiss of life! I can't leave him but I need to get communication to bar staff or other doormen to get an ambulance. There's only one thing for it; I grab his arm and turn into Christopher Dean while he's my Jane Torville as I drag him, bolero-style, across the dance floor! I'm not sure what marks we got for that, a couple of 9:9s I think. I know he ended up with a few marks from the dancefloor, a neck brace for a few weeks and he moved on to another club after that

19

episode. Yep, he left with his 'king of the dance floor' reputation intact. Not sure if he became dancefloor champ at his next club, just know I've never seen anybody attempt a backflip like that again...... THANK GOD!

3.

Citizen's Advice

One Saturday night, we were on the door at this night club. It was okay to work; not too bad for fights as nightclubs went in those days. There were three of us started work there at 9 o'clock then a 4th doorman would come in about 11.30 after he finished working at the pub he'd be working earlier in the night. Three of us were ex-boxers and the 4th doorman was just one of those nutty, scarred-up, Freddy Kruger-faced, psycho, crazy, mental, no fear horrible bastards. It was back in the days before doorman badges, security checks and all the rest of it, so Freddy Kruger was good to work with. He had previous for armed robbery, ABH, GBH, warehouse jobs; just about everything, I liked him, though; a really nice bloke. Just don't cross him or his brothers.

Throughout the night, we had a steady flow of people through the door. The usual Saturday night crowd, a few slappers a few scrappers, a few dappers and a whole lot of mix and match people, which is what you want. The time arrived for the 4th doorman to turn up, which, as usual, was about 11.30ish. We had a quick chat and giggle about if he'd been busy at his pub earlier, then on with doing the door at this night club. After about an hour, it was seemingly going to be a quiet night, and when I say quiet, that means about two fights. That's why earlier on I was explaining it was okay to work there because most nightclubs in those days averaged about 6 to 7 fights a night, and, every couple of weeks, a big kick-off, you know, proper wild-west style, with glasses, bottles, chairs and some stiletto's thrown in for good measure; and that was just on the kids night, the little blighters! So, after about an hour of being on the door, a taxi pulled up outside the club, and out fell two couples, absolutely inebriated, or as we would like to say, 'absolutely wankered'. Up walked the women towards the door looking rough and ready, fire in their eyes and ready to fight the world and probably win too. Staggering behind them, the two blokes were all joyful and triumphant.

"Sorry, ladies; not tonight," I croaked out, ready to shimmy about on my feet because I just had this 6th sense about these two women. Also, I never win with women - when it comes to a row, an argument, fisticuffs, cooking or debating a situation, women always do me in a battle of tongue fu. Women just beat me every time, no matter what. "What the fuck do you mean, not tonight?" screamed one of the women like a raving mental banshee. "Not tonight, ladies. You're pissed," replied my mate. "You've had enough," he said, all nice and calm for a Freddy Kruger lookalike. Now the blokes have got to the door, swaying about all over the place, looking at us with puppy dog eyes. I'm feeling a bit sorry for these two blokes because it's blatantly obvious who the Old Bill nick when they turn up at their houses for domestic violence. I was also thinking, 'I bet they turn up mob-handed to arrest these women'.

"I'm going to fucking Citizen's Advice about this, you fucking idiots. I'm not having it!" screams the larger of the two women. I would describe her as the bigger older sister of the Honey Monster out of the Sugar Puff adverts. "I'm not fucking having it. Right, I'm off to do the doorman; fuck them!" Fucking what? Did I just hear that right - she's going to do the doorman?

With that, bang! She's only banged Freddy and he's gone down onto the deck, but he's not out of it. I am though - I'm in bits! I've lost it, laughing out loud. Whoosh! The Honey Monster has only taken a swing at me and missed, thank God. I mean, I've had some clouts in my time but just didn't fancy one from the Sugar Puff lady, especially if she knocked me out - reputation and all that! The bitch spun around and went for Freddy again, but he ducked and dived, did a quick Ali shuffle and he was back through the club door, slammed it shut and bolted it with me outside. Yeah, that's right; me outside (nice one)! Now I was not bothered about the blokes because they just stood there lighting up a cigarette each, but I've got start moving about, dodging Sugar Puff lady, wondering if her mate is going to give me a sly dig with a stiletto. All the time this was going on I can see my three so-called 'partners on the door' looking out the window, absolutely pissing themselves laughing at me running round like something out of a Benny Hill sketch with these two nutty women chasing me, all the time screaming on about going to Citizen's Advice for not letting them into the nightclub. Fucking Citizens Advice? All I wanted was for that fucking night club door to open!

Eventually, the two women got knackered. Right; here's my chance. I made a lifesaving dash for the door; BASTARDS didn't open it for me! Starter's orders were off again and I was in front by a stiletto's heel. You may ask what their two blokes who they arrived with were doing. Well, let me tell you; they were doing the same as the nightclub doormen - stood there laughing at the whole scene that was happening! Also, people were turning up to enter the nightclub and they were having a right old laugh at what was occurring.

So, after what was probably seconds but seemed like hours to me, the two women were knackered again. As they bent over, panting for breath, I looked at the window where the three other doormen had their faces squashed up against the window and I gave them the 'I'll fucking kill you if you don't open the door this time' look. So, I went for it - the door opened and I made it inside. As soon as I got inside, we all just looked at each other and cracked up into fits of giggles. Moments later, outside, we saw a taxi dropping off some more punters for the nightclub, and into the empty taxi got the two couples with one more shout from the Honey Monster, and she wasn't shouting, 'Tell 'em about the honey, Mummy.' No! She shouted, "You will be hearing from the Citizen's Advice Bureau!" Silly cow. So, the weeks passed by; usual shit every weekend. Never heard anything from the Citizen's Advice Bureau. Then one Saturday night, Freddy turned up to start his shift. "You won't fucking believe what happened to me the other day," he said with a smirk. "I went down the Citizen's Advice with the missus to do with a dress or something and, as I walked in, I only clocked that big nutty bird, the Honey Monster!" I started thinking back to that night and then laughing to myself. "So, what did you do?" I asked, because I know him and I know he wouldn't have let what happened that night go without some kind of repercussion.

"Simple. I went back later when they were shutting up shop. As she turned round from locking the door, I let her have a straight right; knocked her clean out, the big fat cow!" he said with a big daft grin on his face.

"You had better watch yourself now; the Old Bill will be after you," I said.

"No, they won't; I was dressed as a woman when I did it. They'll think it was some female citizen who was advised wrong!"

4.

The Pheasant and the Stripper

Sometimes we used to do the door on strip nights. I only ever did one strip night for ladies and that was enough. It's not the feeling of inadequacy because there are four or five geezers in the pub with muscle-ripped bodies, tanned, good looking and hung like a Cleethorpes donkey on a sunny day; nothing at all to do with that; it's the women again. They go nuts after these strip shows! During the only one I did, I had to lock myself in the cloakroom with the manager of the club and some male bar staff! I don't know what happened to the other doormen that night, but I heard they went with a smile on their faces and with their boots on! So, there you go, the one and only time I did a ladies' strip night and, as usual, the women got the better of me again; story of my life.

I didn't mind doing the strip nights for the men; I mean, it's not like the men are going to try and rip my clothes off at the end of the night, is it? Unless I get the wrong night to turn up and it goes totally brokeback. Not that I'm into these strip nights. They don't do anything for me. I would rather be working the door watching a football match, but anyway, each to their own. I tell you I see some sights on these strip nights! I mean, some of the local councillors, politicians and so-called pillars of the community… all I want to say about some of these guys is that with what I saw them get up to and do, they were lucky that mobile phones with cameras or video weren't about then or their careers would have been finished; either that or some people would be getting rich on a brown envelope.

One night, there were these strippers turned up and they didn't bother with the old warm-up act and then put your money in the pint glass for extras. These strippers went straight at it! There were four men on the dance floor from the start, laying down, sat in chairs, tied up; it was fucking mental. One of these strippers was a bit chubby and she was doing cartwheels, handstands and flip flaps (excuse the pun), doing the sex acts with everyone. We only found out after the show the reason she was a bit chubby was because she was 6 months' pregnant! I couldn't get my head around that one; still can't, to be honest.

So, the other stripper was a real slender piece, getting on a bit and really well-spoken; couldn't get my head around that either. She reminded me a bit of that Lorraine Chase off the television. So, at the end of the show, we were having a chat with them and they offered us the extras free of charge. All the doormen refused. I think what swayed it was the fact of just seeing them with half the club stuck up them on the dance floor, but the manager of this certain club fancied a bit of Lorraine Chase, so he asked us all to leave the room. With a drunken smirk on his face like he's just pulled her, he then locked the door. Now he thought he was sorted but what he hadn't realised was that we could get through to that room via the DJ box. So, off we went! Me, the DJ and one other door staff member climbed over the DJ box and opened the partition door that led us behind the bar in the room where the Lorraine Chase lookalike was sorting out the gaffer with a bit of head. We all looked at each other and got the giggles at the carry-on.

The pair of them were making porno noises; you know the sort - 'mmm', 'ooohhh', 'aarrr', 'yum, yum' and all the rest of it, then we saw something the three of us couldn't believe. The gaffer of the club only went down on her! Are you kidding me? She's just had half the club stuck up her and some not practising safe sex, if you know what I mean. With that, the other doorman just sticks a pheasant up in the air; yeah, you read that right - a fucking pheasant! Now, what got me at the time was where had the pheasant come from? Then the doorman starts talking in a really high-pitched voice, making the pheasant bounce along the bar:

"What's all this then? What do we have here? Can I join in?" said the pheasant, a bit like a feathered Joe Pasquale. Well, the prozzie jumped to her feet and knocked the gaffer to the floor.

"What the fuck is all this sick shit going on, you fucking sick bastards?!" she squealed. We were just rolling about the floor in hysterics. The gaffer saw the funny side and cracked up, so then the elegant naked Lorraine Chase lookalike prostitute lost it. She charged over to the bar and picked up the pheasant by its legs and started swinging it around like a nutty 12-year-old child swings a pillowcase around in a pillow fight. Let me tell you this - I don't know if pheasants hurt when they're alive, but I know they fucking hurt when they're dead. She was whacking the four of us with this pheasant, screaming plum-in-mouth abuse, so we all made for the door like the Three Stooges and his step-brother. We managed to get the door open and run through to the other bar where the after-party was taking place. After-party my arse! A couple of strippers, doormen and councillor pervs! They all stared in shock as we ran through the bar with panic-stricken faces, being chased by a semi-naked Lorraine Chase swinging a pheasant around and screaming abuse! I haven't got a clue what they must have been thinking at the time. Well, me, I carried on running straight through that bar and made my way to the next fire exit, smashed into the long safety bar that releases the double doors to let me out into the nice safe cold night air. I could see the safety of my car in the distance, so in a matter of seconds, I was in my car and started the engine. Whoosh! The front door opened and the DJ jumped in. "Let's get the fuck out of here!" he panted out in a breath which was a mixture of exhaustion and laughter, then whoosh! The back door opened and the gaffer jumped in looking like a red Sitting Bull, as the fucking mug has a feather in his hair. "Let's go, let's go, let's go! She's gone fucking mental; I reckon I turned her on too much!" he says laughing. The timing of that statement just killed me. We managed to get out of the street without seeing Lorraine. "Take me home; I'm whacked. I'll get the manager to lock up," the gaffer said, slumping down in the back of my car.

Loads of questions were asked by people after the events of that night and between friends, doormen, DJs, ladies of the night and councillors, I would answer as honestly as I could or wanted to, but the one thing that always stuck in my mind that I could never truthfully answer, probably because I didn't know the fucking answer, was this - where the fuck did that pheasant come from?! I never, ever found out. I mean, who the fuck brings a pheasant to a nightclub, who the fuck brings a pheasant to a stripper show and what kind of weirdo would bring a pheasant to a stripper show at a nightclub? Fucking weirdos! The one last question I have for anybody reading this who was there that night is this.... Where the fuck did the pheasant disappear to?

5.

Bruce Lee on the Door

I was working this venue down the beachfront; nothing special, to be honest with you, it was fucking shit. Years before it had been the in place to be, then the gaffer who had it had moved on to bigger venues. I think it was on about its third attempt of someone trying to make it a busy place again. It did alright but it was just shit because at that time on Friday and Saturday nights, working the door, I was used to working really good venues, like raves, nightclubs or trendy bars. This place had a shit DJ, shit bar staff and a shit gaffer. You couldn't really say that the trade was just passing trade because this bar wasn't even on the main drag for your usual weekend revellers. Anyway, it was a wage for easy money so you can't complain really. The manager of this bar was Italian. He didn't own it, he just ran it, but he was a complete knob. Fuck me, this guy said he was in the mafia, knew Don Corleone, he told us he ate olives, pizza, pasta and drank red wine every day. I thought he was full of shit myself. I don't even think he was Italian! I reckon he was Egyptian or Turkish or that way on if you know what I mean.

We used to work the door with three of us. You could have got by with two working the door, but if anything kicked off you were isolated from the other bars around you, so they asked for three doormen when it first opened and we kept it to three. You always did that wherever you worked, because once they saw you could run a door with fewer doormen than they were paying for, that was going to be you doing that venue all the time with fewer door staff; more profit for the gaffers. Fuck them. I'd rather put the money in my mates' pockets than theirs as you will see later on in this story.

So, New Year's Eve was upon us and we were struggling to get a third doorman to work with us. If that happened on the busiest night of the year then there was no way we would be working with a third doorman for the rest of the year, so me and my mate were ringing round asking anybody and everybody to work the door just to keep the number of doormen to three. We were asking grannies, trannies, traffic wardens, lollypop ladies, bus drivers, we were asking old friends, new friends, bent friends, straight friends and Channel 4 friends, but we are getting no joy. One of my old school friends turned up at the venue and I started telling him the story of trying to get someone to work. Straight away he offered to do it, but here's the thing; he was one of my best mates through school and after. We had done some naughty things together growing up which I won't go into. He did a few stints of porridge and then he joined the TA, and I'm very proud to say became a different person, but he's no scrapper/fighter; he's never worked the door before. My mate is a comedian. He could laugh people out the door; he could make them love him then charm them out of the door, oh, and he's only 5ft 6" tall. But fuck it; he was up for it and we were struggling so the job was his, a bit of double-time money for him.

New Year's Eve arrived and I went to pick him up. His missus was not too happy about him doing the door but I told her he would be alright as we never got any trouble in the place

I was working at the moment. This was near enough the truth, because this place didn't get a lot of trouble and, like I said earlier, you could get by with two doormen, but fuck them, if they want to pay for three doormen then they can. So, on the way to work, I said to my mate (let's call him Wayne);

"Look, the gaffer here is a cunt. He thinks he's God's gift to women and thinks he's something out of The Godfather. He's going to start asking you questions because you're not very big for a doorman."

Before I could say any more, Wayne interrupted me; remember, my mate was funny and a charmer.

"Yeah, fuck René or Renato or whatever you call him, I'm going to tell him I'm a Kung Fu master and that I've trained with the Shaolin Monks!"

As he was saying this, he was contorting his face and lifting his right arm with his hand in a finger-clenching position, which he later told me was a snake number 5 death grip and he'd got it from mambo number 5. 'More like fucking Chanel No5', I thought.

We arrived at the venue and I let the head doorman know what the score was and that Wayne was a Kung Fu master who trained with the Shaolin Monks. He just cracked up; I mean proper lost it. Straight away, Italian Tony was over shaking hands and asking who Wayne was, so the head doorman took him aside and started talking to him out of earshot. Then you could see Tony look at Wayne, his lips moved rapidly, the head doorman nodded as in the manner of a reply, then Tony's eyes opened wide. In my head, Operation 'DON'T LAUGH, FOR FUCK SAKE' kicked in.

So, the venue started filling up nicely through the night and Don Phoney Tony won't leave Wayne alone. Tony has gone for it hook, line and sinker. Now, I've done a bit of the old martial arts - Matty McCourt on YouTube proves that - so I know the difference in techniques. Wayne didn't. He was stood on the door kicking his legs in the air like Basil Fawlty doing the goose walk in Fawlty Towers, then he's crouching down like a wicket-keeper telling Don Phoney Tony how he used to dodge arrows being fired at him. Arrows, my fat arse! He'd maybe dodged darts when we've been in a fight in the boozer! Wait; it gets better. He started rolling around on the floor then jumping up and shouting mad noises and Tony was loving it. So, what happens? After all that bollocks about not getting any trouble in there, we have a fight. To be fair, Wayne got stuck in and it got dissolved pretty quickly, no harm done. Now, I didn't see what Wayne did in the melee, but at the end of the night, Tony pulled Wayne aside, had a quick chat, shook his hand and walked away. That was it; we were done and out of there, double pay, no one injured, luvvly jubbly.

Driving Wayne home, I asked him what our Italian friend had said to him. Wayne replied;

"He wants me to run the door and sack you two. He asked if I could get any friends who had been at the monastery with me." Classic! Absolute classic. Me and my friend left the place after that; nothing like a bit of loyalty between the manager and his door staff. No hard feelings as far as I know, well, I've never woken up with a horse's head or donkey's head in my bed, so the Mafia man must have given us his blessing. He was about as much in the Mafia as Postman Pat.

6.

Battering the Dog

One night on the door, we were working this club; a good place to work, a good crew of lads. You always had to be switched on as it was a busy place. It had a lot of good-looking women coming through the doors, you know, the sort of women who took great pride in their appearance. Well, one of the lads on our crew was a looker - muscles, tan, patter - he had the full package with the women. Speaking of packages, he had one of them also and the women loved him. I wasn't jealous one little bit of the fucking prick. I mean, this guy was cool; he was so cool, he was cooler than an ice cube in Fonzie's fridge freezer. So, he'd disappear every now and then through the night and we would find him outside behind the wheelie bins, in the cloakroom, in dark corners; we would find him anywhere and everywhere, stuck up some tart. I say tart because when you think about it, if they are getting a bit of a quickie in a toilet or DJ box of a nightclub, they don't come into the 'lady' category in my book. I've seen it so, so, so many times. Sometimes, I've had the fella of the woman coming up to me asking if I've seen his loved one. I felt like saying, "Mate, I've seen more than enough of her and her knickers don't match her bra, especially when they are around her ankles," but I would always be nice to the fellas. To be honest, I felt sorry for the fellas most of the time.

So, let's get back to our friend who we will call Casanova. Now, Casanova was married, so he had to use the full list of alibis we all used on the door when getting home late. We used to share an arrest sheet that stated you had been in the cells for ABH. All we did was crumple the paper and smudge it where it said the name and date. The women never checked it; well, mine didn't. We did the old 'car has broken down' routine - after your encounter, you would open your bonnet and dirty your hands with a bit of grease or anything mucky. You got a flat tyre on the way home, you had to stay behind and do a statement to the Old Bill because there had been an almighty fight, you've been down the hospital because you've been assaulted, you saw a UFO, had to give Simon Cowell a lift home and on and on and on. There were loads of different alibis we used, but Casanova had the best alibi that I have ever heard. It's mental, but this is how he told us the events of what happened on his momentous night the week before.

So, he left the club one night and he'd arranged to meet a new notch down the street, out of the way of prying eyes. She got into the motor and they drove off to a secluded spot, neither of them having anywhere to go because they are both married; brief encounters and all that bollocks. They got a little boogie-woogie going on in the car, windows steaming up and all the rest of it; proper session. Anyway, towards the end of the boogie-woogie, there was an accident; let's just say a messy accident, an accident that is going to be very hard to explain to her indoors. I wouldn't know what to do; I'd panic, I'd freak out, but not Casanova. Remember, he's the ice cube in Fonzie's fridge freezer. Firstly, he told the woman to get out of his car, which she was quite happy to do because she was embarrassed by what had happened. Then he drove home.

WHAT? Now we couldn't believe what we were hearing! He'd gone home at 3.30 am with the mess in his car. You're probably saying, "Why 3.30 am?" Well, that's your cut off point for not getting grief off the missus. The club shuts at 2 am, so you have an hour and a half to get your perks; sometimes, if it wasn't busy, you would sneak off earlier and the lads on the door would cover it for you. If you didn't pull, you sat in your car listening to the radio or reading a paper or had a drive around. Sometimes, a drive around town in the early hours of the morning can be therapeutic after a night of booming music and drunks stressing you out. If you went home any earlier than 3.30 am then it would be expected all the time.

So, Casanova went home. When he got home, he decided to take his dog for a walk. Now, you might ask yourself why take your dog for a walk when he's got what looks like a melted Twix stain on the car seat in the back of his car? Well, Casanova was cool and he was a genius. He took the dog for a short walk and when he got back home, he started to beat the poor dog. The dog was yelping and barking and woke up the household, at which point his wife came downstairs and asked, "What the fuck is going on? Why are you beating my poor baby?" Obviously, 'baby' is referring to the dog, not an actual baby. Casanova replied "I've just taken the dog out for a walk and on the way back the little bastard has shit in my car. What the fuck have you been feeding him?" Feeling guilty, the wife said in a croaky voice, "A little left-over Chinese from the takeaway we had earlier."

Casanova, as quick as a flash, jumped in; "It's all your fault then. He's never done it before. You can clean up his fucking mess because I ain't and it fucking stinks!"

So, the smooth bastard only had his wife cleaning up the whoopsie from the other woman at 4 o'clock in the morning. I mean, let's get it right here - I've seen 'HAPPY DAYS' loads of times and even Fonzie couldn't pull that one off, HEEYYYYYYY !!!!!!!!!!!

7.

WPC Pillhead

One night on the door, I was working this nightclub. It was a rave place. I was upstairs on my own until about 11.30 pm, then I would have a partner turn up from one of the local pubs that then used to shut at 11 pm. Every Friday night, this couple used to come up to the nightclub and chat to me. I would tolerate their chatter, bored to be honest. The girl was up her own arse, you know the kind, one of these snobby bitches who thought she was better than everybody else; proper silver spoon bitch. They would stand there telling me what they owned, how much her nails cost, where his fucking socks were made, that they used certain hair products because they were made by an Idol Loon - well I think they said that - like I give a fuck about hair products; I'm balder than a racing car's tyres! But the thing they talked about best was slagging people off. Oh boy, they loved to slag people off, and I fucking hate that in a person. Now you can imagine in a rave club they would never stop slagging people off. People were gurning their tits off, dancing away, sweating their bollocks off having a great night and they would be calling them for doing drugs and blah blah fucking blah. Pair of boring cunts; did my nut more than any drug I can imagine. Like I said before, I don't take drugs; my high is adrenaline.

So, this one Friday night, I was stood at my station watching the punters in the club, and out the corner of my eye I saw the local Posh and Becks walk through the door, so I was thinking, 'Here we go with the local slag fest of people and what they're up to and what they are wearing and how much it all cost'. But this time was different; she came bouncing in the club like a kangaroo on springs and she approached me from my right shoulder, brushed her fit body right up to mine, stood on her tip-toes, put her lips next to my earhole and whispered in a husky sultry tone, "How you doing, Matty?" I couldn't believe it. Something stood to attention straight away and we're not talking soldiers! I turned to look at her and could tell straight away she was off her cake; pupils dilated, rolling of her lips (on her mouth, I'm talking about) and every 5 seconds the puff of breath. Oh yeah, Mrs Bucket, Mrs Prim and Proper was off her rocker. She leant forward again and whispered in my ear, "I've had an E." I thought to myself, 'You wouldn't have to be an egghead to have guessed that one', then she whispered again, "I'm rushing that much I'm nearly coming. I'm horny as fuck and I want you." That was enough for me. I had a quick scout around for her fella and saw him giving it large on the dance floor. Nice one! I grabbed her hand and led her to an old pay booth in the club. Now, this club has 2 floors and the old pay booth was upstairs, nearby where my doorman station was. Daft, really, because you already had your trouble in the club if anybody tried to refuse to pay to come in. So, the new management had put a pay booth in downstairs as you walked into the club so any trouble was sorted out at the door as it should be.

Now, to get into the pay booth upstairs you had to walk through a staff door that led you to the bar, kitchen, offices and DJ Box. I led the girl by the hand; she was puffing and panting and gurning her tits off. I led her through the staff door and to

40

the disused pay booth. I'd got my Sid James face on and I was ready to take a liberty with the posh tart. Well, it's the perks of my job, innit?

"Matty, call back," crackled in my earpiece coming from my radio. "Matty, call back." Fuck sake, I couldn't believe it. I pushed my button and spoke back, "What the fuck is it?"

"Go check the fire exit upstairs, will ya?" came back the reply. Now, this was a regular occurrence. While the club was open in the first few hours, some of the punters knew there was only one doorman upstairs, and we would be relying on the bar staff to keep an eye on the fire exit as well as serving drinks, so what they would do was distract any bar staff working, then open the fire exit to let their mates in. I don't blame them, to be honest; it's the sort of thing I would do before I worked the doors. Come to think of it, I've still done it and will in the future.

"Right, don't you move," I said to Mrs Bucket. 'Bastards,' I thought as I very quickly walked to check the fire exit. I walked through the club of wide-eyed dancers with a pole in my pocket, and as I got to the door, I could see it was shut. Great; that will do me. I radioed down to the lads on the front door to tell them.

"Okay, Matty. Nice one. Go back to your station," came back through my earpiece. 'The only fucking station I'm going back to is a PlayStation,' I thought to myself as I moved through the wide-eyed dancers.

I walked through the staff door to the pay booth door, placed my right hand on the door handle and started to unzip my fly with my left hand. As I opened the door, what greeted me was shocking. You could have knocked me over with a fried onion ring. Miss Prim and Proper had a member of the bar staff on top of her, gyrating away while she was dishing out moans of ecstasy. One of the DJs from the club was fondling her breasts with his hands and his mouth and to the side of them was some punter from the club getting wanked off by her. The light from the hallway didn't even startle them. As I opened the door, all three lads just looked at me and smiled. I just shut the door, re-zipped the fly on my trousers and walked off back to my doorman station, absolutely gutted at my bad luck.

Now, about ten minutes passed and it was playing on my mind. I mean, Miss Prim and Proper was a tidy bit of stuff. So, out of curiosity, I went back to the pay booth to see if she was alright. I opened the door; I couldn't fucking believe it - she was at it again with some other member of the bar staff! I shut the door and returned to my doorman station. With that, Miss Prim and Proper's other half walks up to me. He was on a bit of a comedown now so, obviously, he was going to be wondering where his missus was. "Oi, Matty, you seen my missus?" he shouted, spraying spit and sweat all over the place. Funny that, because she was doing the same, spraying spit and sweat all over the place! "Na, mate, I ain't seen her for a bit; you tried the back room?" I asked him, thinking I hope no one is in her back room, the fucking nymph. So, off he goes, dancing and bouncing up and down trying to find his better half, or worse half, whichever way you want to look at it. Funny they were both bouncing.

The other doorman had now arrived to partner me. "Everything alright?" he asked. "You're fucking kidding," I replied, so I told him what had gone on. He just stood there with his mouth opened in half a smile. "Look, we need to get her out the pay booth before the owners downstairs find out, or we'll all be sacked," I told him. Just as I was saying this to him, over his shoulder I saw the staff door open and a bow-legged girl walked out with her hair all over the place and her clothes looking dishevelled. With that, the boyfriend walked up; "Oi, oi, sweetheart, where have you been? I've been looking for you all over. I've had a really good night, have you?" he said to her. "Yeah, one of the best ever," she replied and then slung a wink at me. She asked her fella if they could go because she was not in the mood for anymore dancing. "Yeah, sure babe, let's go. I'm in the mood for something else," he said. All that went through my head was, 'She's had quite enough of that for one night'.

Now, this couple had been coming to this club for at least 6 months, every Friday without fail. I never saw them again at the club after that. The next time I saw her was two weeks later on a Saturday afternoon in the local shopping precinct. She had her hair cut in a different style and was wearing glasses. She did see me but made out that she hadn't seen me. I only saw her a couple of times after that; she was wearing a police uniform. She had become Old Bill, which I think suited her personality, if you think back to how I told you she was with punters in the club. I don't know what her call sign was but if they're ever stuck, I think WPC Jizz Bucket might be appropriate.

8.

The Gaza Strip

One night on the door, I was working this bar/nightclub. It was part of five new venues that had been opened down near the shopping precinct. When they built this complex, I think the idea was for people to go and do their shopping in the afternoon, then retire to one of these venues for a spot of lunch or maybe a coffee and a light snack; lovely. Then on a night time, people could come to these places for a few drinks and sit outside in the moonlight by the riverside chatting about business deals and who was fucking who in Emmerdale Farm; lovely.

That was the idea and, to be honest, it was a good one that should have worked - apart from the Emmerdale Farm bit; should be chatting about EastEnders. What they ended up with were five venues where, in the daytime, most of the alcoholics hung out because they were doing cheap deals on the booze. With the alcoholics came the druggies which brought the shoplifters, so, in the daytime, it was where people went for their cheap shopping and talked about who was fucking who in the high-rise flats; lovely. Then, on a night time, because they were still doing cheap offers on alcohol, everybody went there; coke dealers, young guns, plastic gangsters all congested into this strip of bars, and by the riverside in the moonlight, the only business deals getting done were dodgy ones, and the people getting fucked were the ones getting chucked into the

Riverhead. Thus was born, and I claim the honour of giving it this legendary name, 'THE GAZA STRIP'.

So, I was working this bar/nightclub and the place was hard work. If you looked in the dictionary for stressful, this place would get a mention. The music was loud; underage chavs trying to get in; old hard men who had seen better days but were now past it because of the workless days sat in pubs telling stories about barroom brawls when they were younger. We had it all to deal with.

This one night, we turned away two underage drinkers from the door. They were okay about it. They knew they were underage but had a bit of friendly banter with me and my partner and then walked off towards other bars on the strip, probably calling us 'FAT OLD BALD BASTARDS' under their breath. As they were walking, one of them was stopped by two policemen and cornered against the railings of the walkway that stopped you from falling into the river. Now, I couldn't hear what was going on but the young lad had changed from being a funny cocky character, like he was with us, to a very aggressive young man. His face started to get contorted with aggression. As he was demonstrating with the two policemen, his friend was bouncing about trying to intervene. As he was doing so, two other policemen come to the aid of their colleagues, to move on the friend who was bouncing about like Tigger on a trampoline. As they were trying to move him on, two other young lads got involved. I'm guessing they were mates of the two young lads, or probably just two young lads who hated authorities and wanted to have a go at them. The Gaza Strip was full of people with that mentality.

Now, it was turning into a bit of a farce, like something out of the Keystone Cops. While all this was happening, obviously, you had a drunken crowd gathered, cheering, jeering and having their say about the cluster fuck that is occurring in front of them, so rightly, one of the policemen got on his radio and, in what seemed a panic, asked for back up, which was right because it was getting out of hand. Within minutes, at the end of the Gaza Strip, a police van appeared and out jumped four policemen on a mission to help their colleagues. They pushed their way through the crowd like bulls on a stampede, which ain't a bad description, judging by the size of their arses. So now, the four new policemen have achieved the great status of upsetting the onlookers, therefore the drunken banter turns to verbal abuse which is returned by the police. Then the new arrivals call for back up because the crowd are revolting, and I'm not talking about revolting in looks; we're well past that stage. At the other end of the Gaza Strip, in the distance, I could see another police van turn up with blue lights flashing. I couldn't see how many police got out of that van, but it was a lot judging by the way the crowd was parting to let them through. At our end of the Gaza Strip, another police van pulled up. This van was 'The Dog Section' - the four-legged kind, better known as canines, not the WPC section, and behind that van, another van.

I was stood on the door, watching all this chaos, with what punters were left in the bar. They had their faces pushed up against the window watching all this happening. Now, with the police having good numbers, the panic had gone from their faces and the confidence had appeared. They started making arrests and wrestling with the onlookers. One of them sprayed some CS gas at an onlooker, but obviously, he hadn't been trained in the art of using CS gas. As soon as CS leaves a tin, it expands, so he's also hit innocent onlookers and fellow police; now they're all screaming. Just in front of my feet fell a policeman, struggling with a man.

"Give us a hand here, mate. I'm struggling," he shouted up from the floor to me. I just looked down at him, shrugged my shoulders and replied, "I don't think so, mate".

Let me explain the reason why I did this. Some months before, I had been at Crown Court charged with 3ABHs, for helping out somebody in need, which is what I was always taught from a very early age; always help people out in need. You know the story, about the good Samaritan and the geezer at the side of the road, my brother's keeper and all that kind of stuff, and right before my very eyes was the same scenario going on. The police were outnumbered, just the same as the people I had helped out, yet I ended up in Crown Court on my own, the only person from a big affray being charged. Bollocks; I ended up with 2 not guilty verdicts and a hung jury on the 3rd ABH. God bless the jury for making the right decisions. People would pass me in the street and say, "Oi, mate, you got off with them charges." I would reply, "I never got off with anything; I never did anything wrong; justice prevailed."

Back to the Keystone Cops caper. Now, this chaos had been going on for about 20 minutes from the start of the first two coppers trying to arrest that young lad. There had been more CS sprayed; fuck me - if they'd sprayed much more I dread to think of the size of the hole in the ozone layer! The police dogs were going mental, barking at everyone and anything, and so were the canine variety, but they were now beginning to gain control of it all. A few more policemen had arrived from somewhere- not sure if they parachuted in or swam underwater down the Riverhead - as people started moving about and returning to their night of drinking, dancing, snorting, arguing and fighting. Me and my doorman partner started talking about how easy the police have it compared to us on the door. I mean, we had to charm those lads away from the door with a bit of banter, but if it had turned naughty, we couldn't call for back up, use handcuffs, truncheons and spray CS gas, or call for the dogs to be sent in, unless we used a couple of the barmaids to bite them; come to think about it, that has happened before.

At the end of the night, I had my customary free pint to wind down and once again talk about the goings-on from earlier on that night. I finished my pint and walked off the Gaza Strip and across the road to where my car was, parked in a D.I.Y. store car park. As I took out my keys to unlock the remote alarm on my car, I heard the sound of a diesel van coming up behind me; not just any diesel van, but a police transit diesel van. You may ask how did I know, but trust me, anybody who has dealings with the police will tell you, one of their vans has its own growl, not like any other transit diesel van on the road.

Then from behind me comes the voice,

"Oi! McCourt! What the fuck was that all about earlier on, not helping me out, you wanker?"

I turned round and saw the copper who had been laid out on the floor earlier.

"You having a fucking laugh? After what you did to me earlier on this year, you lot trying to stitch me up, for helping somebody out?" By now, the van had stopped to the side of

48

me. The copper was sitting in the passenger seat with his window down, and the side door of the diesel van was open revealing two coppers sat there ready to pounce. I started thinking to myself, 'I am fucked here. I'm either getting a slapping or set up for assault on a copper.' The CCTV for the car park was blocked by the positioning of the van, but then I heard an angel's voice, a saviour;

"Oi! You said you would give me a lift home and sort me out!" It was one of the barmaids from another club on the Gaza Strip. I let out a huge sigh of relief.

"Yeah, hurry up then, for fuck sake, girl!" I shouted back to my guardian angel. In one second, I seemed to catch the eye of all the policemen sitting in the van and smiled at them.

"You've been lucky tonight, McCourt, but your cards are well and truly marked now, son," said the copper in the passenger seat as the van started to drive away. 'Yeah, no fucking shit,' I thought to myself. I owed that barmaid and I made sure she got sorted out, and as for the police marking my cards, they weren't lying. As the song goes, 'I fought the law and the law won'. The outline of this story was written from my prison cell where I am serving 6 months for a fight on the door. Not that the people I was fighting with were bothered; it was the police who pursued it all the way, God bless 'em.

9.

Shithouse Decorator.

One night on the door, I was working this venue in the summertime; not a big place, but it was spread over two floors, averaging about 150 people downstairs and about the same upstairs. We used to work the door with two of us. There was very rarely any trouble in this venue and if there was, it was very minor. it was a good place to work, on the main drag of bars and clubs, with two of us on a Friday night and three of us on a Saturday night. Something strange that was happening quite regularly in this venue was that somebody kept smashing the mirror in the upstairs toilet and other daft bits of vandalism. I never get why people do that kind of shit in bars. I get ripping the condom machine or cigarette machine off the wall, I even understand them pinching loo roll and fittings, but I can't get my head round smashing up the toilets for no reason; fucking weirdos.

So, with this going on, it made our job a little bit busier for some time. We were having to check the toilets more than normal during our shift of door work; a doorman will usually check the toilets for drug use, mischief and of course, people having sex. It's very rare you'll catch a doorman having sex in the toilets; if they've got anything about them, they'll use the disabled toilets - more room in there and you can lock it down properly from the inside so you don't get disturbed. We won't go into all the extra fittings in a disabled toilet; what do you think I'm writing here? 50 Shades of Door Work?

My partner at this venue was Dave and we had been partners for about 7 years. We worked and managed a number of venues together. He was a good lad, 100 % 'had your back' material. We both belonged to the same Amateur Boxing Club. Dave had his ABA coaching qualifications, so we used to do a lot of corner work together. I would hand up the spit bucket, water bottle and whatever else he required. These were good times and we travelled around the country doing this.

One Friday night, we were working the door and we found ourselves with a problem. We were going to be a doorman short the next night. We had asked all the doormen we knew, but it was summertime and they were either working somewhere else or at a wedding, engagement, stag party or barbeque. Summertime always gave you these problems, and like I say, once you worked a venue with fewer doormen than you'd used before, the owners would be on you like vultures to keep to that number of doormen all the time and save themselves some money in wages. They don't give a fuck about your safety; I've never met a landlord who does; never.

Dave and I were stood on the door, scratching our bald heads, wondering what we were going to do when up walked a friend of mine from my daytime job. Yeah, that's right; my daytime job. I've always had two jobs. I like to work; it's good for the soul and I'm a soul man. Now, this work friend of mine could tell a story. He was from another town and he had done everything - black belt in ju-jitsu, karate, judo, Ker-plunk and backgammon. He had scored hat-tricks in every game of football he played, always got a 9-dart finish and 147 when he played snooker; you understand what I'm saying about this character - told more lies than a Pinocchio family reunion! He served in the forces (that was genuine) but he told everybody Rambo was based on him. Dave, my partner, liked him and loved his stories, so as Rambo walked up, Dave asked him, "Hey, George, you ever worked the door?"

"Yeah, course I have," he replied in a John Wayne drawl. Even his walk changed as he answered Dave. Of course, I knew he would say 'yes'; I was waiting for the story that he had worked with Patrick Swayze at Roadhouse.

"Brilliant. You can work tomorrow night, George, and help us out. We're short; start at 8, cheers." Boom! Just like that; that's how Dave was; very forceful, single track-minded. George had no chance to reply; he did change his walk, though. The boy who cried wolf sprang to mind.

The next night at 8 pm, George showed up on time, head shaved to the skull, wearing a black jacket that looked like it had been pumped up with air. His upper body looked so big compared to the rest of his body - let me put it in context - his head looked like a pea on a drum. Dave and I had already arranged the night before that, at all times throughout the night, George would be stood with one of us and not left on his own.

The shift went well with the usual steady flow of punters in and out of the venue. Dave and I were taking it in turns wandering around the venue checking the toilets, always making sure George was never on his own. With about an hour of the shift to go, I was stood upstairs on my own looking out of the window at all the punters below having a great night out enjoying themselves, when one of the barmaids walked up to me and told me I had better go downstairs as it looked like there could be some trouble brewing. I walked down the stairs and made my way to the front door to find Dave and George squared up to three men and a lady, but unlike the film of the same name, this film would have been a horror if this lady had been in it. She was one scary-looking bitch with language that was scarier.

"That's him!" shouted one of the men, pointing to me. "That's the one who did me!" Now, I didn't have a fucking clue what he was on about. I'd never seen him before in my life, but I could tell by looking at the state of his clothes and face he had been in some kind of fight.

"Wait a minute, you just said it was him," said Dave pointing towards George, "then you said it was me, now you're saying it's him? You wanna make your fucking mind up!" I was stood there, none the wiser to what the fuck was going on. I asked Dave what the score was, and Dave explained that the three men and the lady had walked up to the door and accused the doormen of doing over the one who was in a mess. When he finished telling me, I stepped towards the men and explained that I hadn't been in any confrontation that night and that there hadn't been any trouble that night in the venue. Just as I finished being diplomatic, trying to dissolve a potentially explosive situation, the lady stepped forward, pointed her finger at me and switched into Jeremy Kyle contestant mode; "I think you are a fucking liar! You look an 'orrible bastard who would do something like that, and my friend ain't no fucking liar! You're a cunt! Wotta you gotta say to that?" she barked at me in a gravelled smoke-abused voice.

"You fancy me, don't you?" I said back to her, smiling. With that, she did that Tasmanian Devil twisting thing they do in

Bugs Bunny cartoons and the three men had to restrain her from ripping my head off.

"Look, sweetheart, I've been here all night. If you and your friends think I've assaulted one of you, go get the police, have me arrested, take my clothes away for blood stains or any other kind of DNA, no problems!" Now, I'd said this to her in a cool, calm, soothing voice manner, and BOOOMMM!!!!!! I put a spell on her! She smiled at me, her body and attitude relaxing instantly and she turned to the three men and said, "I don't think he did it."

"What?" screams the assaulted man. "I don't think he did it; in fact, I don't think you've been in here tonight," she said back to him. I was beginning to like her now and that gravelled voice I hated turned into one of those sexy, husky voices, like that bird out of Cagney and Lacey. Funny how things can change like that. Well, now they started arguing amongst themselves and started to shuffle off down the street away from the venue. I thought to myself, 'Nice one. They're obviously all drunk and have got the wrong venue.' As they got further into the distance, Dave laughed and then said he had something to tell me.

Earlier in the night, Dave had been checking the upstairs toilets and noticed that one of the cubicles was locked but there were no feet on the floor, so he went into the cubicle next door, stepped on the pan and pulled himself up on the partition wall and looked over the top into the locked cubicle. To his amazement, he saw a man stood on the toilet pan lid, having a shit on the cistern! Dave jumped down from the toilet and kicked open the locked door of the cubicle. As he was doing this, just by chance, the owner of the venue walked into the toilet. Now, the gaffer of this pub was mental and well-known around town for being not right in the head. He would drink more vodka in a week than the population of Moscow! In all the time I knew and worked for him, he was never sober, no matter what time of day or night it was. He made Oliver Reed look teetotal. So, the gaffer, thinking it had something to do with the vandalism of the toilets, set about bashing up Dave's friend from 'The Mile-High Shit Club'. Dave started to drag the owner of the venue off the man before he got a proper good beating. He managed to throw the man out the back-door fire exit upstairs. While all this was going on, George and I didn't have a clue and Dave thought it best not to tell us until the end of the night.

"Fuck me, Dave! How can they mix us up with the owner of the pub?" I asked him in amazement. Let me explain why. All three of us working the door that night had shaved heads, two of us had goatee beards, all three of us were dressed in a black jacket, black trousers and black shoes, all roughly about 30 years of age. The owner of the pub had a full head of grey hair, he was clean-shaven with a face that was worn through nicotine and alcohol abuse, he was wearing a light blue shirt and light blue jeans and brown shoes, and to top it off, he was about 20 years older than us. That, without doubt, was the worst case of mistaken identity I had ever come across. Anyway, fuck them and that filthy bastard; they'd gone now.

Half an hour later and we were asking the last of the punters to drink up so we could get ready to close, as we were not very busy now. Dave and I were collecting glasses and helping out with the cleaning of the venue. We'd left George on the door on his own for the first time that night. Then, all of a sudden, there was a loud thud and a commotion coming from the doorway. Dave and I ran towards the door to find George crumpled up on the floor, knocked out, and the lady from earlier on making her way off down the street through the night-time punters! It gets worse - as George was laid on the floor, a bunch of our workmates walked past and all started pointing and laughing at him. Dave and I couldn't believe it! We hardly ever got trouble in that venue, apart from the nutty owner who used to talk gibberish to us. Dave and I felt a bit guilty about leaving him on his own for those few minutes, but that's probably about the length of time we felt guilty for; a few minutes. Obviously, after that night, George never worked the door again. He never told us any more bullshit stories. Funnily enough, he never bored the lads at work with his bullshit stories and, within six months, he had moved away from our area never to be seen again. As for the Lady with the husky voice - I'll let you work that one out for yourselves.

What about the vandalism? Well, a couple of weeks later we caught the culprit. Dave and I were working the door when a young lad came up to us and told us that someone upstairs was smashing up the toilets. Dave and I raced up the stairs and burst into the toilet to be met by a young lad and a middle-aged man. Now, straight away you're thinking the same as we did - the young lad had done it - but the middle-aged man's knuckles were bleeding. No brainer; we got him, plus the young lad shit himself and grassed him up. Now, I'm not one for handing people in to the police. In 22 years of working the door, I've never handed anyone in to the Police, so we gave the man a choice- pay for the damage and be on your way, or wait here - we will get the police, you will be arrested, go to court, get a fine, court costs and a criminal record. With that, he started crying and telling us he didn't have any money and didn't want us to call the police because he was a school teacher. You just can't help some people, can you? Here was a middle-aged man out on a Saturday night and he's trying to tell us he hasn't got any money? In my mind, I'm thinking, 'This cunt is mugging me off and taking my kindness for weakness.'

"OK, mate, no probs; have it your way." I looked at Dave and said, "Keep him here. I'm off to get the vodka zombie; he can deal with him", meaning I was off to get the owner of the venue. Minutes later, I returned to the toilets with the owner. The teacher was still crying like a baby and talking nonsense. "There you go, boss, he's all yours," I told the owner. "There's your toilet vandal." Me and Dave walked away from the toilet block to the sound of violence, or if you like, the sweet sounds of vengeance.

Funnily enough, the toilet block never got damaged again, and the middle-aged man? I only saw him again a couple of times in the local paper; things to do with education. I wonder if we'll ever see him on University Challenge or Eggheads? When asked what his specialised subject is, he replies 'Decorating Toilets'.

10.

Dark Destroyer

One night on the door, I was working this venue, a nice bar on the main route of bars round our way. My doorman partner was more than just someone who had my back; he was my ex-boxing coach and a very good friend of my family. He was a fitness fanatic, good to have in a tear up, a good amateur and professional boxing champion in his own right. His attitude to working the door was the same as mine; we both preferred to deal with confrontations through communication, humour, charm and a bit of the old street psychology rather than getting physical, and 90% of the time, that was good enough. Over the years, a lot of my partners were of the boxing fraternity or were martial artists and had that same kind of attitude to working the door and dealing with the public, which was good and what I wanted to work with, rather than some egotistical leary prick who inflames situations.

So, Stu and I were working the door one Saturday night when a friend of ours, John, walked up. Now, John was a very charismatic man; so charismatic he could sell you smoke-damaged fire alarms. A budding entrepreneur at the time, he had his fingers in more pies than a baker. Stu and I liked John a lot; he always had a funny story to tell. He used to put on dance nights, or raves if you like, once a month. They were very popular, and sometimes I would go down and help out on the door at his raves when I finished working at other venues. At other times, I would just turn up and do a bit of socialising, and throw a few shapes if I was in the mood.

John started telling us about his next rave coming up and that it was on Boxing Day Night and that he had a big-named DJ turning up. As he was telling us this, he had a massive smile on his face. Now, don't get me wrong - John was always smiling, but this time his smile was like a Cheshire Cat with dental implants, a smile that would make Simon Cowell's smile look like old man Steptoe. He told us he had booked Nigel Benn, the former world boxing champion, and that he had all his security sorted out for the night but he wanted me and Stu to be Nigel Benn's private bodyguards for the night. He continued to tell us that Benn was booked for only an hour and detailed what he would pay us for the hour. Let's put it this way; he was going to pay us treble our wages for working the door for the night for one hour's work. No hesitation, Stu and I agreed to do it, shook his hand and thanked him for giving us the job. Best of it all was I would have done that work for nothing, just for the prestige and honour of being the great Nigel Benn's bodyguard. I was a mahoosive fanatical fan of his when he used to box. I went to loads of his fights. I was borderline stalker material! Unless it was a present from my daughters, that was the best Christmas present I was getting that year, no doubt.

Boxing Day arrived and all I could think about was that night when I was going to be doing my Kevin Costner bit and Nigel Benn was going to be my Whitney Houston. I spent the day with my family eating turkey buns and watching the usual shit on TV, then about 6 pm, I nipped into my garage and had a massive weights session followed by a few katas and stretching to loosen up, then went back into my house and got showered and shaved ready for the night's work.

Stu and I arrived at the venue at about 9 o'clock. The car park was huge and it was already full. We both drove around the car park trying to find a space. There was nowhere to park so we pulled onto the main road and parked about a quarter of a mile away from the venue. We walked back towards the venue and walked up to the front door where John was waiting for us, suited and booted, looking dapper and smiling as usual. A big queue was formed outside and the place looked packed inside; no wonder John was smiling - nice little earner for him.

"Looks like a good night, John," I said, reaching my hand out to shake his.

"Yeah, of course," he replied, smiling. "Benn has just rung me. He'll be about ten minutes. We'll bring him in through the back door and straight to the stage. He's going to be here for 45 minutes now, then he's off to Leeds. I'll still pay you the same cash though."

"No probs," replied Stu.

Now, the good thing about this venue was that Stu and I had worked there on numerous occasions before, sometimes for the venue, sometimes privately for whoever had hired it out for the day or the night. Both of us had boxed there, attended several boxing events there, and I even had my wedding reception there, so we were well familiar with the layout.

As we stood waiting at the back doors with the music booming behind us, waiting for Nigel Benn to show up, I started telling Stu a story about when I worked in Germany. One time I ended up in the local police station sharing a cell with five other British lads. One was this cockney lad called Derek and he started telling me stories that Nigel Benn was a smoker and popped E's (ecstasy tablets). I never believed him and told him nobody as fit and as strong as Benn, who was an awesome fighter, would pop E's, let alone smoke. As I was finishing the story, a big red pickup truck pulled into the car park; it looked a bit like that truck out of the Fall Guy, remember that show about the stuntman? Fuck me, he drove into the car park and pulled straight into a parking space. Well, to be honest, where the fuck did they come from? You couldn't park anywhere 15 minutes before; unbelievable! It was obvious to us Benn was driving the truck, either that or Moses, the way he parted the cars to get a space. Stu and I walked towards the pickup, and as we did, my hero appeared from the driver's side and, from the passenger's side, appeared his wife. Benn fixed us both with that stare he gave many an opponent when he was in the boxing ring. I swear to God, I thought I was going to end up with a cauliflower ear just by his stare.

"Alright Nigel?" said Stu, reaching out his hand to shake his, and with the speed of one of his knock-out punches, he grabbed Stu and gave him a hug and started laughing, then looked at me and grabbed me and gave me a hug.

"How's it going, guys?" laughed Benn.

"'Ere, let me get your records, mate," I said, grabbing hold of the box of records from the back of the pickup. All four of us began to walk towards the back door of the venue. As we did, a toothless scummy mummy, E'd up and all sweaty from dancing, well, I think from dancing, who knows, came running towards us and started screaming, "Nigel, Nigel, geez a kiss!" At that point, Nigel looked at me and Stu to defend him. I looked at Stu then held up the box of records and gave him a nod to say, 'You deal with her; I've got my hands full'. I don't think he was pleased with the deal, but anyway he tells her, "Not now, love, he's busy; maybe later." I felt like adding, "Yeah, when you've put your gnashers back in". We got through the back door of the venue and made our way to the stage. As we got onto the stage, the legendary DJ, Dean Baker, was waiting with some of his friends, and so began a lot of back-slapping, hugging and shaking of hands.

Within minutes, a local DJ by the name of Flynn grabbed the mike and started to get the crowd going with his Emceeing (microphone control) about Benn being in the building. As usual, the crowd responded to Flynn and then the chimes of Big Ben began to ring around the venue. The crowd were going mental, and with that, Nigel Benn began his set of music for the next 45 minutes. Things were going okay - I was watching the crowd for any nutters, streakers or gummy mummies, then glancing my eyes back to where Benn was stood and then at Stu. Benn had to keep bending down behind the podium that was supporting the decks to get his retrieve records out of his box, then one time he did it, he had a crafty puff on a cigarette. I couldn't believe it! I was in shock; he did this a couple of times, then on the third time of bending down, he flicked his hand towards his mouth in the style of a Red Indian like out of the old cowboy movies. I turned and looked at Stu and said, "He's just popped a fucking pill! I don't fucking believe what I'm seeing here!" I felt gutted seeing my all-time boxing idol do that. Benn carried on with the set and finished it off in good style. The crowd loved him. He packed away his records, then we got through all the usual hugging and hand-shaking shit again. Benn, always the gentleman, accommodated everyone with the pleasantries, then we left the stage and shuffled through the crowd. Again, handshakes and kisses to all his adoring fans. Benn was laughing and loving it! I was switched on like Blackpool illuminations; my eyes are all over and I was ready to die protecting my man. Wasn't too sure what to do if the gummy mummy came though; probably fight her off with a toothbrush. As we left the building, I looked at Stu and said, "He seems alright, don't he?" "Yeah, don't look bad for someone who has popped a couple of pills," Stu replied, laughing,

"What the fuck do you mean, a couple of pills? I only saw him pop one!" Stu couldn't stop laughing at me. We got to Benn's motor, wished him all the best, had a quick picture taken with him, (which has special place among my boxing memorabilia) and stood back ready to watch him drive off.

Now, as we all know, Nigel Benn is a former World Boxing Champion, but fuck me, when it came to driving, he must have got his licence out of a lucky bag! Firstly, he backed the car up and smashed into the car behind him. He opened his door, popped his head out, looked at the damage and started laughing. He shut the door, pulled forward on an angle and hit the car in front of him. Then he backed up again on a slightly different angle and hit a car next to the one he'd previously just hit, then pulled forward and drove off. As he turned left in the crammed car park, he clipped a car on his left-hand side forcing Benn's car over to the right where he smashed into two other cars. Stu and I both stood there astonished at the mini demolition derby we had just witnessed, then Stu came out with, "Can you imagine if somebody had got out of one of them cars all aggro, giving it large, only to be confronted by Nigel Benn?" We both just cracked up laughing and I thought to myself, 'What a great night. I'm never, ever going to forget this'.

Three boxers on Boxing Day Night and one of them off his box.

We went back inside the venue, collected our money from the still-smiling John, and left. One of the main reasons for leaving was we didn't want to be around when the car owners returned to their cars to find them all bashed up.

Years later, I met Nigel Benn when he was touring the country talking about how he was a born-again Christian, telling about his days of drug abuse. After he had finished, I was chatting to him and he said he could not remember if he had been to my town before. I pulled out my phone and showed him pictures of us together on two separate occasions. He laughed and said, "See, I told you I was out of my head. I couldn't remember if I had been here before." I started laughing with him and said, "Yeah, well, I remembered you being here before, that's why I left my car at home!" He looked at me, puzzled, as we posed for our picture. That was my third time of meeting Nigel Benn; always a pleasure. Nigel Benn - as much a legend out of the ring as he is in it... GOD BLESS HIM.

11.

Die Hard

One night on the door and I was working this bar. It was December time; to be more precise it was 'Caarraaazzzyyy Friday'. The police call it Black Friday - well, they would do, wouldn't they? They're a fucking racist institution. Now, if you don't know, Crazy Friday is the last Friday in December before the big day, when just about every man and his dog are out on the piss, (or if you want to be politically correct, every person and his pet). People who got out once a year. All year round they are sane, normal, straight-headed law-abiding citizens, who stay in every night to watch the soaps and do a bit of bobbing sex every other weekend on a Saturday night. (Bobbing sex - refer to FUBARA Poetry book to see what it means). Now, I've seen this year in, year out; they get a couple of sherbets down their Gregory Peck and then want to fight the world and his pet. Men will turn into Rockyrambovandammejohnwaynebruceleeschwarzenegger with a twist of Shaft, hard as fuck, God's gift to women, invincible warriors. They will know every gangster that has walked the face of the earth; they will be related to the flavour of the month gangsters, have a hidden cache of arms somewhere, because they will be coming back to shoot you, that's unless they put a contract out on you with the Cartel, Mafia, Posse, Firm, Gang or local Youth Club! Yep, all year watching action movies and now, in their head, they have become that movie, and this is just the men who work in the library.

As for the women - 'WOWZERS!' When they're pissed on Crazy Friday and get all aggro, they will be married to Britain's Strongest Man, their brothers will be world boxing champions, their cousins run a Shaolin Temple of Kung Fu down in Torquay, their Father will run some terrorist organisation, and with a couple of Dry Martini's down their neck, they will turn into Uma Thurman's character out of the movie 'Kill Bill'! CRAZY FRIDAY - the most stressful night of the year for Doormen, Bouncers, Rescue Services and Takeaways, without a doubt.

Now, normally, after working this bar, I would work somewhere else for a couple of hours to top my money up, and I knew without a doubt on 'Crazy Friday' there would be a mega choice of venues to work, because nearly all venues take on extra staff for this night and unusually, a lot of staff ring in sick. Like I say, this wasn't a normal night so I had no interest in working anywhere else after my shift. I just wanted to get the fuck out of Dodge alive.

The bonus of this particular night was that the bar I was working at had been open all day and had a good day's takings by the way of an unexpected turn-up of about 100 contractors who had finished early that day for Christmas. It had been a rainy dismal day so the contractors stayed in the bar. The gaffer of the bar put on free food, made the pool table free for the day, and every now and then would sling in free shots. I think if he could have got some strippers down there sharpish he would have done, so, of course, most of the contractors bedded in the bar for the day, and of course with the bar being busy and bouncing to the usual year in, year out, fucking annoying Christmas tunes of Wizard, Elton John, Paul McCartney and whoever else comes on at that time of year, it attracted other people who had finished early for Christmas. When I arrived for work at 8 pm to start my shift, the owner of the bar was smiling from ear to ear and started telling me what a great day's money he had taken over the bar. The bar had been packed all day, there had been no trouble and the contractors had nearly drunk the place out of his order of alcohol for the weekend in one afternoon. He continued to tell me he was going to be shutting bang on time that night for two reasons; one, he had to be up early in the morning to try and get more alcohol in for the weekend, beg, steal or rob, and the second reason was he wanted to get through the night with no incidents, which I thought was a good idea. Every time there is an incident at a venue, it is logged with the authorities so that when you come up for renewing your alcohol and entertainments licence, it makes the process more difficult for renewal, or the brown envelope thicker for certain persons to approve renewal. I thought, 'That will do me; nice one. 'I'm a doorman; get me out of here'.

Behind the bar were a couple of barmaids who were good girls. We all know the reputation of doormen and we all know the reputation of barmaids, so when you put the two together you know you're going to get one hell of a banging night. Well, one of them I fancied the arse off (to be honest, all of them). She was fit, and oh my gosh, didn't she know it! She used to wear outfits that would show off her toned midriff, she was pretty and had a great personality. I would always flirt with her, and tonight, with the bar shutting right on time, it was looking like the night for some nocturnal activities, before my 3.30 am cut off point of having to be home. So, we exchanged some words, flirts and innuendos and arranged to meet at her house after work.

Last orders and then time had been shouted in the bar. It had been a good night with no trouble; of course, it was stressful but that was expected on 'CRAZY FRIDAY'. Throughout the night I had refused the usual offers of working other venues. I only had one thing on my mind that night; I left work and drove to the barmaid's house. She was sat outside in her car waiting for me. We got out of our cars at the same time and smiled at each other. The anticipation was more electric than a lightning bolt in a power station! We walked up the garden path and entered the front door. I thought to myself, 'This is going to be 'man the battle stations' in the hallway.' As soon as we walked through the door, the heat and smell of Christmas hit me from the lovely cosy terraced house. We walked down the hallway and entered a double room to our left, and there, in the corner of the room, was a beautifully decorated Christmas tree with white lights gently flickering and the smell of cinnamon filled the room. I lost the horn.

"Do you want a coffee"? she asked. "Yeah, go on then," I replied. As she walked into the kitchen, I couldn't help myself but admire her slender-shaped curvy figure; the horn reappeared.

"Nice house," I shouted as I picked up the remote control for the television and did a backward star-shaped free fall into the big soft comfy couch.

"Yeah, nice innit? Gotta give half to my ex-husband, though, and my kids are at my mum's." I vaguely heard a voice say this from the kitchen, but it was wasted; it fell on deaf ears.

I had found the Sky Movies Channel, and Die Hard was on! Now look, Die Hard to me at that time was one of the best action movies I had ever seen and it's set at Christmas time and the first-ever time I saw it was at Christmas time on a VHS recorder when I was still living at my mam's. I love Die Hard and The Lethal Weapon movies of that time; love 'em.

My barmaid friend re-entered the room from the kitchen with a cup of coffee in each hand. I barely noticed her and did not have a clue what she was waffling on about. I was lost in the film. She sat next to me on the big comfy couch and her perfume smelled so sweet. I didn't flinch; she handed me a cup of tea and whispered, all sultry like,

"Sorry, am I disturbing you?" I laughed and apologised. "I'm sorry, but I love this film. You don't mind if I watch it, do ya?"

Out of the corner of my eye under the flicker of the Christmas tree lights, I spied a tin of Roses chocolates. "Can I have a chocolate, please?" I asked.

"I was saving them for the kids for Christmas, but go on then," she huffed with a fake smile. (What the fuck is it with people saving it for Christmas? It was four fucking days away! They all wait until the big day and then think they've got to eat it in that one day; mugs).

So, I'm there watching the film, laid on the couch, shoes off, eating chocolates, putting the empty sweet wrappers nicely on the floor by the tin. I don't want to put them back in the tin and get them mixed up with the unopened sweets, do I now? That would be out of order! The film was coming towards the end, so I checked my watch and there's still plenty of time to have some fun until my 3.30 am cut off point. All of a sudden, my barmaid friend got up off the couch and walked towards the kitchen. "Would you like another coffee?" she shouted back towards me. "Yeah, go on then." I thought, 'That's bad timing - the film is nearly finished; mind you, a swill of coffee could help rinse away some of this toffee stuck in my teeth.' I stood up from the couch and straightened myself up, gave my shoulders a shrug and thought to myself, 'Fuck the coffee; fuck the barmaid.' I started my strut towards the kitchen, but as I was on my third step, my ears pricked up as I heard the end credits music of the 'Die Hard' movie; a presenter spoke and said,

"Stay right with us for the second part of our double-bill of Die Hard movies tonight; Die Hard 2." I couldn't believe my good luck, or bad luck, whichever way you want to look at it. I started to moonwalk across the carpet back to the couch and as my heels touched the couch, I did my free-fall back on to the couch and virtually landed in the same place as before. My mind was working overtime on how I was going to explain to my coffee-making friend that I wanted to watch 'Die Hard 2'. As she walked back in the room with a cup in each hand, she had a look of disappointment on her face. "I suppose you're going to want to watch this film as well, aren't you?" She sighed, handing me the coffee.

"I'm sorry but I love Die Hard 1 just as much as Die Hard 2." She was probably thinking, 'I'd love to die hard or do anything hard'.

We both sat there watching the movie, me buzzing at the action movie and her not buzzing due to the lack of action due to the action movie. When the movie finished, she made her move; she was on me like a gazelle.

"Hang on, hang on, I've got to get off," I said. I had just about reached my 3.30 am cut off point.

"What the fuck do you mean, you're off? Are you fucking serious? you come round here, lie on my couch, drink my coffee, eat my kids' chocolates and then tell me you're going without sorting me out, you bastard?"

I thought to myself, 'She's lost it'. You get to see these signs. I better not mention the ham sandwich she made me and forgot to mention on her tirade.

"Look, you know the score; I got to be in," I told her as I started putting on my Crombie. "I'll come round another time if you like?"

"Fuck off, you bastard! If you ever come round again, I'll hide the chocolates and check the TV Times!" she screamed at me, folding her arms in a huff.

As I walked down the short garden path towards my car, I got the giggles, but I didn't dare let her see my face. I heard the door slam behind me and some obscenities being shouted from behind the door. I pulled a Lambert and Butler cigarette from the inside pocket of my Crombie coat, lit it, took a draw on my cigarette, looked at her lovely warm cosy terraced house, exhaled the smoke from my mouth and whispered,

"Yippee-ki-yay, motherfucker!"

12.

Guy Fawkes

One night, I was on the door at this venue, a very nice, very trendy bar and restaurant. I ran this venue right from the first night of opening, and I kept it tight on dress code and age. I kept it strictly over 21s, no tracksuits, no baseball caps, basically, a chav-free zone. It was a great place to work; it had great regular drinkers and diners coming through the door every Friday and Saturday night. It was the first venture into this sort of business for the man who owned it and he just left me to run the door. He became a good friend of mine and my family, and we would all go round to his house for Sunday dinner and parties and he and his wife would make a fuss of my children. Good times! He also helped me out in some investments and other money matters, and he remains a good friend to this day.

This venue was way off the main route of the local drinking scene, but what was good about it was that it was between two sets of main drinking areas in town so it was like a halfway house if punters were going from one drinking area to another, and from a doorman's point of view, you got to see someone in the distance and judge if they were pissed, or as we would say at this place, inebriated. People always do it - walk to a bar or club and as they get near the point of entrance, they straighten up and do their best to act sober, and if they pull it off, our problem is inside the venue and not outside on the door where it is easy to deal with, or should I say, easier.

Because this bar was located halfway between the other two drinking areas, it wasn't that clearly lit up. You had your street lights and a flow of traffic going down the main road, but the buildings either side of the bar were shut and the front of the building had a balcony from the first floor which covered the top of the entrance and this ran all the way down the street from one corner to the other, making the pathway a lot darker than the other side of the street. If you stood across the road and looked at the venue I was working, the two buildings to the left were not in use and both had dark roller shutters covering their shop fronts. Then, you had a narrow street to the side of them that was about 15ft across, which was dark. After that, on the next block, there were about five or six buildings which were all shut at night and that block was also dark. To the right of the bar when looking at it, there was a pizza place next door, then a line of buildings that were also shut at night, until you got to the end where there was an amusement arcade and a fish and chip shop. What I'm saying is it wasn't very bright around there; a bit like myself, not too bright.

One dark, wintery Friday night, me and my partner Matty were working on the door. We were steady, as usual, when out of the darkness a fellow comes stumbling towards the door. "Sorry, mate, not tonight," I said, putting my hand across the door. "You've had too many."

"No, I haven't; I'm not even drunk," he slurred. "No, sorry mate," I repeated

"Why?" he slurred once again. "Because you have had too many," I repeated once again.

"Why?" he slurred again, "Cos you've had too many, mate. Go try somewhere else; not tonight," I repeated, and this was the intellectually enthralling conversation that went on and on. Now, some people would say, "Why didn't you fuck him off, or just stop talking to him?" Well, I like to be polite. My mam brought me up that way. The way I looked at him was that he was just a harmless drunk; annoying but harmless. Plus, like I said, we were having a steady night, so it broke up the boredom for a bit.

Matty turned to me and said, "Do you want a cup of coffee?"

"Yeah, go on, mate. Get me a black coffee, Dalton style." (little roadhouse joke there) "I'll be alright with him."

So, Matty goes into the bar to get us some coffees. As soon as he goes in, my new drunken friend is at me with questions.

"Why can't I come in? Why you being a wanker? Do you think you're hard?"

Well, that was it now because I'd been alright and polite with him. Now it was what I call 'tongue fu' time; you might call it sarcasm.

"Look, mate, you're not coming in. We don't have an ugliness-only night and you're more pissed than Olly Reed who's been at a free bar all day. Just go somewhere else," I said to him with an air of menace.

"Fuck you and fuck Beryl Reid! I'm coming in and you're not stopping me."

As he took his first step forward, I swept his front leg away, grabbing his jacket lapels at the same time, sending him off balance to my right. As he slipped to the floor, I still had control of the manoeuvre and, as quick as a flash, he went to sleep. Within seconds of this happening, I heard the door of the bar behind me open. I didn't even have to turn; I knew it was going to be Matty. As I laid the Oliver Reed wannabe on the floor, I spoke out to Matty, "I didn't touch him."

"Yeah, I know. I saw it all; so did half the bar," replied Matty.

"'Ere, look, move him over there out the way; it don't look good for the bar," I said, so we dragged Sleeping Beauty to next door's shopfront. He could get a decent sleep there - it was darker. By the time we had finished placing him next door, his jacket had risen above his head and now he was snoring. It gets better; then his mobile phone starts ringing with 'ding ding, bom bom, bram bram," that fucking annoying Crazy Frog ringtone that only weirdos had. So, we left him there, snoring away, and every couple of minutes a Crazy Frog ringtone would sound. Matty and I decided to finish our coffees then wake him up, bless him.

On a Friday night, as regular as clockwork, five local businessmen used to visit our bar. They were proper Jack the Lad sorts. I'd known them at that time for about ten or twelve years and everybody liked them. As they approached the bar, a young lad of about 14 walked up to our friend, Sleeping Beauty, to see what he was all about, laid on the floor. As he did, one of the businessmen chucked him a coin and shouted, "Nice one, son. Best Guy Fawkes I've seen; like the noises!"

"Cheers, mister," shouted back the lad, picking up the coin, then with that, he said to the other businessmen, "Have you got a penny for the guy?" Of course, they chucked some coins because, like I say, they always pleased people. Well, that was it; the young lad was away with his nice little earner, and Matty and I were in hysterics and loving the cheek of the young lad. After about twenty minutes, I walked up to the young lad and told him I was going to have to wake up Sleeping Beauty before he got hypothermia or such like because I'm nice like that.

"Okay, no probs. I've made a nice few quid," said the young lad. He told me his name was George, then he shook my hand and cleared off into the side street. I thought to myself, 'What a nice lad'. I leaned over Sleeping Beauty and gave him a few gentle taps on his jacket in the area of his head. "Oi mate, oi mate, wake up, wake up, c'mon mate, wake up." There was movement from underneath the coat and his head popped out, a bit like a turtle's head popping out. His eyes were all bleary; he looked like he'd been asleep for 12 hours. He reached out his hand towards me, so I grabbed it and pulled his arm towards me. He rose to his feet; "Cheers, mate. What happened?" he said in a groggy voice.

"You've been asleep, mate, snoring your head off. We could hardly hear the music in the bar with your snoring!" We both started to laugh. He shook my hand and told me he was sorry about what happened, but I told him to forget about it. That's it; job done. Got a friend and not an enemy; bit of the old psychology.

The next night, which was the Saturday night, I was working with my partner Dave. Like I've said before, we'd worked together for years and boxed together. We started at 8 pm, and as we began our shift, I started telling Dave about the night before and all the antics, and we were both having a laugh about it, when I heard a voice from behind me; "Alright, mate?" I turned around and saw the young lad from the night before, propping up a stuffed Guy Fawkes against the roller shutter of the shop next door. "Haha! Alright, George? Back to earn some cash, are we? Nice one, son!" As the night went on, we had a steady flow of customers and young George had a very steady flow of coins being chucked at him. When it got to 10 pm, young George told us he had to be getting home because his mum would be worrying. He offered to buy me and Dave a bag of chips each for keeping an eye on him; we both refused but thanked him for the offer.

"Just out of curiosity, George, how much did you make tonight?" Dave asked him. When he told us I nearly gave up working the door there and then and started doing my own 'Penny for the Guy' routine. Let's put it this way, we were on good money at the time working that bar and he had taken just over double our wages and we still had another two hours to work that night!

Young George appeared for the next couple of weekends doing his 'Penny for the Guy' routine. He also appeared for the next couple of years. We used to keep an eye on him to make sure he was safe, and no, we never took any money or bags of chips off him. He was a nice kid and every time I watch the TV programme Dragon's Den, I keep expecting him to turn up on it saying "I started out in business with my Guy Fawkes".

13.

Super Gran

One night on the door, I was working this venue on the main route of pubs and clubs around our way. It was a good place to work; busy, hardly any trouble, done for about 12 usually, which meant I could go to work another venue or go visiting friends for a cup of coffee until my 3.30 am cut off point to get home. Now, because this venue was on the main road, you were constantly chatting to people, all sorts of people, not just drinking punters. It was enjoyable and made the night go quicker. Just round the corner from the venue was a bingo hall, so every Friday night, about 9.30 pm, the main road would become full of pensioners leaving the bingo. The street turned into an invasion of extras from the television programme 'Last of the Summer Wine'. The old dears would walk past us on the door and have a bit of banter with us. Usually, we'd say, "Any good tonight, dear? Maybe next time, eh?" They'd reply with the usual, "No good tonight but when I do win, I'll let you know and you can take me home!" All harmless fun. Usually, after the Blue Rinse Brigade had passed, there would always be this old dear come driving down the pathway on her electric scooter. She would always stop for a quick bit of banter as well, telling us about her ailments and how close she had come to winning the National, (I think she meant the National Bingo Prize; I don't think she had run Aintree, not with those legs, anyway) and then she would be off on her way. Like Moses parting the Red Sea, she would part the stream of punters walking down the main road, and they always respectfully had the courtesy to move for her. Luvvly Jubbly.

One Friday night, I was on the door of this venue and it was raining cats and dogs, or to be P.C., it was raining felines and canines. It was still a busy night with a steady flow of punters moving about from bar to bar, when, from around the corner, came the tide of pensioners with their multitude of different-coloured umbrellas. I thought someone had spiked my coffee as I started to trip out at all the colours and designs. It was like a 'DEE-LITE' music video. As they got close, the usual banter was exchanged, but more quickly that night because of the weather, then along comes the granny racer on her scooter, all geared up with plastic coverings all over her scooter. To be honest, it looked like a used condom on wheels coming down the street! She stopped briefly to exchange pleasantries and drove off.

Now, my contraception, sorry, conception of these electric scooters is, you got one if you couldn't walk or you had trouble walking or you were obese and liked to drive around theme parks, especially Disney ones. That's what I always thought. Well, our granny racer had driven maybe 10 feet away from our venue when a gang of three young lads of maybe 18 or 19, and weighing about 10 stone wet through, appeared next to her. One of them decided to jump on the back of the scooter for a free ride. He did this laughing and cheering to his mates, and they were laughing and cheering back and some of the punters in the street were laughing at the boy's actions; to be fair, it was funny to see. Then, all of a sudden, the electric scooter came to an emergency stop. The lad jumped off at the same time as one side of the scooter's plastic cover was flipped up to reveal a Nutty Nana - we've gone from granny racer to Nutty Nana - and she was giving the young lad abuse and what for. It was so bad her Granny would have been turning in her grave or tomb. After she had finished telling the young man where to go and what to do, she replaced her plastic covering and continued to drive off, so, once again, the young lad hopped on the back of the scooter to the laughter and cheers of the passing punters. Now, me and my partner on the door (Dave H) have seen enough and started making our way over to the scooter to have a word with the young man, when suddenly, the scooter stopped again and the lad jumped off. The plastic covering got flipped up like before, but this time, Nutty Nana jumped off the scooter and now became Super Gran! She took a couple of strides towards the young man then started to hit him with her handbag. The whole situation seemed to go into slow motion to me, (spiked coffee?) Super Gran was swinging her handbag and the young man was leaning back trying to dodge the blows, all the time laughing and screaming out, "I'm sorry, I'm sorry, I'm sorry!"

Then, our new-found Super Gran started screaming back at him, "You little toerag! I'm a pensioner; I can hardly move, let alone walk!" Unbelievable.

After a few seconds but what seemed like hours, we stepped in to stop the bag assault; I mean, she could have been up for assault the way things are nowadays. As I stepped in, the young man moved away and Super Gran caught me a beauty right on the jaw with her handbag! I didn't go down, but if I had, I would have blamed the spiked coffee for my legs giving way; reputation and all that bollocks. In hindsight, that was the best thing to happen, me catching a belter, because the gathered crowd started laughing, so did the young man and so did Super Gran. Super Gran apologised to me, but I told her it wasn't a problem. I found it quite funny that I'd been done by a Granny and knew I was in for some grief about it from other doormen and friends. As Super Gran walked back to her scooter, the crowd started cheering and gave her a round of applause. She started waving and geeing them up - fuck sake, I was surprised she never did an Ali shuffle! She took a bow, hopped into her scooter and drove off. I was half expecting her to pull a wheelie!

So, like most places, most people do routines on their nights out, and now every Friday night at about 9.30 pm when the Bingo kicked out and the last of the Blue Rinse Brigade disappeared, down the pathway would come the town's new-found celebrity, cruising along on her electric scooter. As usual, people would move for her, but now they would have a chat or sling in a nice bit of commentary to her, so she started dishing out a semi-royal wave to people. Super Gran started decorating her scooter; somebody one night gave her a Super Gran sticker and I loved it. Something so good and funny could come out of a bit of mischief by a young man. I think that the last couple of years of Super Gran's life were probably made very happy by those events making her a local celebrity. God Bless Her.

14.

Undercover Old Bill

One night on the door, I was working this rave. It used to be a once-a-month gig for a mate of mine; He paid me well. The score with it was that the council insisted on him having licenced doormen, so he would hire four or six of his own doormen and I would provide myself plus three other doormen, just to keep it all looking above board for the council and the owners of the venue who he rented the room from. Now, the venue was an okay place, I suppose; it had a couple of ground-floor bars and function rooms, and upstairs, one huge room, a big dance floor, a big bar situated in the corner and a stage at one end of the room. Funnily enough, it was the venue where I had my last ever boxing match. Because the downstairs was always open and, at that time, quite busy at weekends, they had their own doormen working there. They were known to me; one was an old-timer who had been doing the doors for a long, long time, who I had respect for; he was called Pete. The other doorman was an old friend of mine from my Martial Arts days called Paul. He went on to do a bit of pro boxing. So, whenever we turned up to work these rave nights, there was always professional courtesy exchanged between both sets of different doormen.

One night on the door at one of these raves, we were working away when the doormen from downstairs came up to see us, but instead of there being their normal two doormen, they had four and two were women. Let's change doormen now to door personnel. My friend Paul was leading the way and spoke out.

"Alright, Matty, we've come to give you a hand."

"With what?" I replied. "We're doing fine as always; don't need you, mate."

"Well, the gaffer of the venue wants to do searches, that's why we've got the women; nothing personal," said Paul.

"Fucking nothing personal, Paul? I run the door up here and you lot work downstairs; it seems a bit personal to me!" I was saying this through gritted teeth, not wanting any trouble. With that, my mate, whose rave it was, took me aside and explained to me that it was okay for them to do it.

"Okay, fuck it, let 'em," I said.

So, as the night went on, they were doing their searches, and the space outside and on the stairs was getting backed up because the silly bollocks had got them taking off their shoes and socks, doing twirls, shaking their clothes about and jumping up and down! I was thinking to myself, 'These poor fuckers are going to be knackered before they get in there and do any dancing!' Now, I know Paul and his team think they were doing a good job, but let's be honest, once that started, the word would have got round, so the punters would start popping pills before they came into the venue, or would be stashing their stash where the stash and the sun don't shine.

Eventually, the queue died down. The place was full and it was the usual gurn fest of dancing and good music. Usually, everyone will blend into the darkness and flashing lights of the dance floor, but for some reason, just in front of me were three characters who didn't blend in. Two were men and one was a woman. The two men just didn't dance right. They were at a

83

rave but dancing like those fucking student types at an R.E.M. concert; you know what I mean - all floppy-armed and looking to the sky like spaced-out zombies. People at raves are spaced out but they stare at you. They've got that 'I'm gonna fucking kill you!' stare while they tell you that they love you. These two men also looked older; it just wasn't right. As for the woman, she could dance and was pretty and she looked the part, but one thing which bothered me about her was she had this backpack on that looked like a sheep. At the time, they were fashionable with children, not with grown-up ravers, especially a fit-as-fuck raver who looked like she could be a raver in bed; rave off.

I was doing my usual - moving about round the venue and having a quick chat with the other doormen - everything was going okay which it normally does at raves. The punters just want to dance! I ended up by the side of the stage with a doorman friend of mine called Gary. He was one of the unlicensed doormen; we used to box together some years before.

"Listen, Matty, I've been having a few drinks backstage with the DJs, is that okay?" He was trying to whisper to me, not that you can find anywhere to whisper at a rave.

"Yeah, no probs, mate. I fancy a drink myself, but I never do when I'm working and I'm driving later," I told him. As I turned back and looked towards the dance floor, I saw the three stooges again dancing near me. I swear to god I wanted to chuck the two men out just for being fucking shit dancers! I turned back to Gary and said,

"There's something not right about them three over there. I reckon they're Old Bill."

"Yeah, a few of the lads have said they're dodgy, and it isn't just their fucking dancing; they keep asking people for Es," he told me.

I walked back to the main entrance and the doormen, sorry, door personnel, were still hanging about. I walked up to Paul and gently grabbed his arm and led him to a quieter spot. I leant my head towards his ear and asked him, "You got summat you wanna tell me about tonight?" I pulled my head back and stared him in the eye. "No, why?" he muttered.

I asked him again, knowing he knew that was not the answer I wanted. "Is there Old Bill in here tonight?"

"Yeah," he said. "We were told not to tell you lads."

"You cunt! I ain't no fucking dealer; you should have given me a heads-up!" Then it all fitted into place; the two women door personnel, the girl with the sheep backpack probably had a radio and cuffs in the back, a Hi-Viz vest, a rocket launcher and all that. I thought to myself, 'I better go tell the other lads.' As I turned round, there were the fucking idiots trying to dance.

"Oi mate, you're wasting your time following me. I ain't no fucking dealer!" I shouted at one of them.

"Dunno what you're on about, mate," he shouted back. "Mate, you're fucking Old Bill, I know you are; you might pull them dance moves off at an ABBA weekend at Butlins, but not here. Juliet Bravo is alright though," I shouted back at him, laughing as I walked off.

The night passed without any trouble and the Old Bill kept a distance after our conversation. To be honest, I don't know why they didn't just leave. I ended up stood back by the stage with Gary. The DJ told the crowd he was on his last two songs then we were done. The next tune came on and Gary was off, jumping on a speaker giving it some shapes. I thought to myself, 'Fuck me, I've been here before; he's been spiked!' "You alright, Gaz?" I shouted up to him.

"Yeah, I'm okay. I need to dance; it's my favourite tune," he shouted back. With that, our two male policeman friends jump on another speaker and start throwing some proper shapes out! Oh yeah, they fitted in well now. The W.P.C. came up to me and asked me to do something, telling me her friends had been spiked.

I told her she should leave them as they were much better dancers now, but I would be willing to help her if she admitted to being Old Bill. She told me she wasn't, so I said, "No probs. I'll do what I can to help you." I didn't know what I was going to do to help. How the fuck do you give First Aid to a pilled-up policeman, especially if they're gurning their tits off dancing like a fucking Teletubby? I went backstage and had a quick word with the DJ. "For fuck sake, hurry up with that last song. I wanna get out of here. The Old Bill are in and they're off their nuts!" I pointed out the policemen to the MC/fucking DJ, whatever the fuck they are called nowadays. He cracked up laughing and gave me the nod, saying that he was going to finish it early. Now, I didn't know what to do. We had to start asking people to leave so we could shut the venue, but now one of the Old Bill has got a whistle from somewhere and is blowing it like one of those bobbies in the old black and white movies, and his co-accused is screaming, "MOOOORRRREEEEEEEE!!!!!!!!" I looked to the female Old Bill and she looked like she was going to have a breakdown, all teary-eyed and just looking in disbelief.

"Okay, okay, we are undercover. Can you please help me?"

Now, I'm not one to see a damsel in distress, so I told her, "Wait a minute. I'll go get something that should help the situation." I nipped off and returned with two yellow glow sticks and handed them to her.

"What the fuck am I supposed to do with them?" she said, looking at me in disbelief.

"Just tell them they're doing a new line in truncheons," I replied. "Look, there's a van-load of your lot parked round the corner. Get hold of them to sort you out." She walked over to her colleagues and started talking to them quietly so no one else could hear; I would say whisper, but as you know, you can't whisper after a night of loud banging music. They started heading for the main exit and as they walked past the doormen, the two men started telling everybody that they loved them and what a great night they had had. They started going on about going to a house party afterwards. The female was getting the hump and pulling some right faces as she tried to drag them away. As they walked off, the door staff were in hysterics! One thing we agreed on was to get out of the area sharpish before the Old Bill parked around the corner saw what state they were in and came back looking to arrest someone for something; you know, a bit of revenge. Nothing ever came of that night; no repercussions from the police; nothing.

One night on the door a few months later, I was working a Saturday night at one of my regular venues, and in the bay window, a woman was sat on her own. She looked fit from behind; the doorman working with me started to tell me she had been there since he started the shift, how men had been approaching her and chatting her up and she had knocked them back. Just as he finished telling me this, she got up to leave the venue. As she approached me, I clocked her face and thought to myself, 'I know her'. As she then walked past, I could see her rucksack; it was a sheep - BOOM!!! I remembered her! She was the Old Bill from the rave. I shouted to her, "Oi Oi!!" She just ignored me and carried on. I suppose there could be a moral to this story - my dear mother used to say to me, "Be aware of wolves in sheep's clothing". Very true, but in this case, I think it should be, 'Be aware of pigs with sheep as their clothing!'

15.

Cheeseburger Brigade

One night on the door, I was working this venue, a great place to work. A big restaurant on one side and a very busy popular bar to the other side of the main doors. I was paid well and it was run very well from the kitchen staff to bar staff, waiters and waitress staff, and, of course, the door staff. Also, the boss of the venue was probably the best gaffer I ever had in all my 22 years of working the door. He would lend me money at the drop of a hat and other sorts of things that took our working relationship out of the normal employer/employee bracket (we won't mention Vegas). But let me tell you this; he was the same as any other landlord I had worked for - he thought he was God's gift to women and he was a sex addict. He was no exception to the rule; he thought he had the right to have sex with every barmaid and waitress that worked for him, maybe even barmen and waiters? Who knows what happened when the punters had gone and the doors were locked and the alcohol flowed. Not that I'm one to start any rumours, hahaha! Also, along with the staff, every landlord thinks they have the right to have sex with any woman (or man) that walks through the door of their premises.

Now, most landlords I have worked for, thinking about it, probably all of them, used the same routine; bit of eye contact, bit of chat and flirting, then the free drinks. The free drinks do it every time. Now, the free drink could be anything from a vodka & coke to a free bottle of champagne. I suppose it depended on the crust of the bust, the size of the thighs, if the flirty was dirty or if the release of the jizz was going to be worth the fizz. Fucking creepy isn't it? But that's what would happen and the ladies let it, then came out with the usual excuses - 'I was drunk; I didn't know what I was doing' or 'yeah, but he told me we were going to get married.' Haha. For fuck sake, some of them genuinely believed they were going to marry the gaffer after a one-night stand, #stupidfuckingbetlynchwannabes.

Now, in this venue I was working at, the landlord had a plan B to the usual landlord sleaze. He would send over food, or he would tell them to come in again and reserve them a table in the bar, he would send over free drinks and let them order anything they liked off the menu for free. Damn, this landlord was so good he even had a plan C to back up if plan B failed! He would use one of the waitresses of the venue to lure them up the wooden hill. Well, she was one of his ex-conquests; well, I say ex, but she still did his mutton dagger for a day at the races or a bit of overtime. I suppose she was a pimpess; she would line up the prey for him, work her magic by getting into the company of these women and then she would be having free food with them. So now, after seeing this time and time again, the regulars in the bar started calling it 'THE CHEESEBURGER BRIGADE'.

Now, the regulars of the bar told us of this name they had given to these goings-on, and all the time, the regulars started dropping funny remarks and innuendos around the landlord and the unsuspecting women. I mean, some of these women would be having a hard time at home or not so hard, whatever the case may be. They would come into the bar, be seated at a reserved table, eat some free food, drink some free alcohol, swan around the bar like they owned it, then get taken upstairs and get hammered by the landlord, then after, shipped off in a taxi back to their old man. It was mental! The door staff and the regulars started calling the bar McShaggings and ShagDonalds! The taxis would turn up for them the same way a car goes through a McDonald's drive-through, and all the time this was going on, the women had the cheek to act like ladies and look down their noses at people. I don't think any amount of Happy Meals could have put a smile on their faces.

Sometimes, contractors would use the bar. Like I say, it was a very busy popular place and they would come and ask us door staff the usual questions;

"What's it like for women in here? Are they easy to pull?"

I'd reply, "Easy to pull? You having a laugh? Don't worry about wearing aftershave in here or expensive clothes, bring in a cheeseburger or some of your packing up from work and you will pull no problem". Now the contractors would look at me all puzzled then probably come out with, "What the fuck are you on about?" So then, I would explain to them what the 'Cheeseburger Brigade' was all about. With that, they would be in hysterics! Sometimes they would even come back with their friends and ask me to tell the story about the infamous Cheeseburger Brigade.

One time, I was telling this story to a contractor and pointed to a table where the Cheeseburger Brigade were sitting. "Watch this," he said as he strutted over to the table. The contractor leant over the table between two of the women, said something and then received a slap to the face. As he walked back towards the door where we were standing, one of the women beckoned over my door partner. As he got to their table, he bent down and exchanged words with one of the women. He turned around and walked back towards me with his hand covering his mouth, trying his best not to laugh. Just as he got level with me, he cracked up laughing.

"What's gone on?" I asked him. He said the contractor had asked if any of the women wanted to go back to his place and if they played their cards right, he would buy them a double Cheeseburger with large fries and let them have a go on his chicken nuggets! Now, you have to remember, these women don't have the foggiest clue what's going on, or about the nickname that has been given to them. These women are more lost than a red-headed clown walking around a KFC.

Some of the men in the pub were thinking of chipping in together (Get it? Chip?) to buy a burger van and place it outside the pub.

There are a few more stories and events that happened relating to the Cheeseburger Brigade. They would come and go and change every couple of months, they'd get their food and get their free drinks, have a nice couple of months of playing "I'm a Celebrity Eater; get me out of here", then go back to their old man. Some would set their sights higher and hang about kebab shops and pizza parlours. And from what I hear around the town, some make their old man dress up in Ronald McDonald outfits to spice up their sex life…… DO, DO, DO, DO, I'M LUVVIN IT.

YOU KNOW WHO YOU ARE!

16.

Pepe Le Pew

One night on the door, I was working this nightclub; a good place, always action of every kind. It was getting on a bit in the night, and sometimes you get the feeling that you are going to have a trouble-free night and this was one of them. I got chatting to this girl; nice smile and red hair, alright really, looked a bit like that bird out of the film 'Pretty in Pink'. We were about 20 minutes from closing time and I was all flirted out, so out came the usual doorman chat-up line;

"Can I give you a lift?"

Sometimes I used to use the line, "Do ya want a lift in my Mercedes?" but that was only when I used to have the company van. Well, I wasn't lying - it was a Mercedes.

She nodded with a smile and said, "Yes!"

My brain went into Sid James mode - 'we're on'.

I turned to two of the other doormen working with me and told them the score, that I was sneaking off, and to cover me so I could gain a bit of time on my 3.30 am cut off point. So, me and my new 'Pretty in Pink' friend sneak off out the back door of the club and down the fire exit to my car. Once in my car, I put on my soul music. Funny; I always had soul music on in my car to help me unwind from the stress of the door, especially a bit of Luther Vandross.

"Right, where do you live?" I asked her. Well, when she told me where she lived, I felt like kicking her out the car. It was miles away - another town down the motorway. It was a fare in a taxi that would feed a third world country! I told her, "Okay, but ya better make it worth my while."

"Yeah, I will," she said with a teasing smile, (Sid James was in my head again).

So, after a while of driving and chatting to each other, and me wondering if I'll need my fucking passport on this road trip, I asked her where she worked and she told me she worked in a canteen on an oil refinery. I told her I knew that place; I'd done some bits and bobs of work on there. Then I started to have a laugh and tease her about the reputation of girls with the men on those refineries. She agreed, laughing along with me and continued to tell me she used to work on a power station behind the refinery when they built that. I never said anything but I worked on that power station! Then, it clicked in my head who she was; for fuck sake, this girl had a right reputation and rightly so - she'd had more cock than a Tottenham Hotspur souvenir shop! Now my mind was racing. What the fuck do I do now? I pulled my car down a country lane and into a little layby by a field, told her to get herself ready, I was just nipping to the boot of my car. So, I got out of my car into the cold, crisp midnight air, went round to the back of my car and popped open the boot. I lifted the covering where my spare tyre was and took out a packet of condoms, secretly stashed there for emergencies, like getting lost in the desert and needing a water carrier (you know the score). Through the back window, I saw my 'Pretty in Pink' friend shuffling about in the passenger seat, getting her kit off and I smiled to myself. I walked back to the driver's side door and put one leg in, half-sitting in the driver's seat, when all of a sudden - BOOOMMMMMM!!!!!! The fucking smell hit me! You've got to remember I'm from Grimsby, worked on the docks as a boy, I know the smell of fish, and we were no way near any docks, trawlers or Dolphin Parks, so quick as you like, I saved myself. "What the fuck's that?" I shouted out, pointing my hand to the windscreen.

"What?" she said. "I thought I saw somebody out there; let's go, quick, and get dressed," I told her, slamming my door shut and, quickly starting the engine, I drove out of the country lane, at the same time discreetly opening my window a little to let in some fresh air! I pulled into a pub car park and parked my car in between two lorries; nice one - secluded and out of the way - but I thought I saw a curtain move on one of the lorries so I told 'Pretty In Pink' this, or as I was now beginning to think of her, 'Clitty that Stink', so she replied with a classic line, "Oh, don't worry, he's not there. I shagged him two nights ago and he was telling me he's going away." As she finished, the smell hit me again. "Look, I think you better get out of my car," I said, trying not to pinch my nose between my fingers.

"What do you mean?" she said, looking at me all gone out. I was wondering how I could put this without offending her; "I'm not in the mood. I've got a headache; something strange has come over me."

With that, she opened the car door and got out, then with both hands, slammed the car door. I thought my side window was going to go in! I jumped out of the car and screamed at her, "What the fuck do you think you're doing?"

"You're not right in the fucking head!" she screamed back. "You're a fucking weirdo!"

"Am I really? Well, let me tell you this, ya fucking minger, you need your fanny washing out with disinfectant... COS IT FUCKING STINKS!!!!!!!!!!" I got back in my car and drove off. As

95

I was driving down the motorway, I was thinking to myself, 'How the fuck did I get in an argument, gone 2 in the morning, with a fucking minger in a pub car park?' I was also thinking I needed to get rid of the smell. I rolled down the front windows of my car and pulled my jacket up over my neck while I was driving; no good - it was still lingering, so I drove to the all-night garage and bought two Magic Tree air fresheners. When I got back in my car, I ripped open the packets and hung both the trees on my rear-view mirror, thinking to myself, 'These trees will need to be magic to get rid of this smell.' I parked up outside my house, got out of my car and hoped that the next morning was going to be a lot fresher. Luckily, the next morning, the trees turned out to be magic and the smell had gone. I didn't have to ring the fumigators out of the Yellow Pages after all.

The following week, I was on the door with the lads. The queue of people to come in was slowly building up. It was the beginning of the night and I was telling them the story of all the antics from the week before. We were all having a laugh about it when I saw 'Pretty in Pink' outside in the queue! "I don't believe it, lads, she's outside," I said, trying to hide my fat head behind my hand. They all started laughing even more now. "What you going to do?" one of them asked, laughing.

"What do you mean, what am I going to do? She ain't coming in. She nearly wrecked my car with slamming doors and stinking my car out!"

"That's nothing to do with the club; you will have to let her in," said another doorman, laughing, which he was right about. I walked outside and looked down the queue. As I did so, she started hurling abuse at me; "Ya fat bald bastard, you fucking weirdo!" Nice one! That will do me. I fire straight back into her with,

"You're not coming in; you're barred."

"For what?" she screamed back.

"For having a smelly fanny! You stink more than Pepe Le Pew after a night on the garlic. We can't have you in this club; we'd have to dish out gas masks in case you fell on the floor and the smell came up from under your dress."

As I was saying this, the queue were laughing at the comedy act of abuse. I could hear the doormen behind me laughing. 'Pretty in Pink' said something to her mate and stormed off, chuntering away to herself.

I walked back in the club and one of the old-school doormen was bent over in hysterics and said, "In all my years doing the door, I've never, ever known anyone get barred because they had a smelly fanny!"

17.

Mick Kelly

One night on the door, I was working this venue. It was my first night; me and my partner had just taken over the place. The venue was about 6 months old and the owner wasn't happy with the doormen he had employed. The DJ had put our names forward to work, so we turned up, discussed business and took over the place. It was a Thursday night, pretty busy, just the two of us working, when up to the door on a pushbike arrives one of the town's great local characters, a well-known face about town and very funny, sometimes for all the wrong reasons. Now, this guy was from the same council estate as me and was a few years older than me, but his escapades were legendary and so, so funny. He would do anything for a dare. In the couple of years before I worked the door, I had been in his company on nights out and always had a laugh. Sometimes he would go in the DJ box in a bar or club and just take over and, to be fair to him, from what I remember he was alright on the decks; goes without saying he was definitely alright on the microphone. From what I've been told, he went on medication for something and ever since then he got worse; worse as in double-dare and double don't give a fuck.

"Alright, Matty?" he said in one of the daft accents he used to put on. "Can me and the bike come in?"

Straight away, I started laughing and replied, "You're alright but you can't bring the bike in."

"Aww, come on, Matty; the bike is old enough. Don't make me go home and get its ID; you're out of order and being vehicilist."

Dave and I were in hysterics and he was loving it! "What the fuck is vehicilist?" asked Dave.

"You know, you've got racists and pacifists and all kinds of fists, well, you not letting my bike in is vehicilist; he's my best mate!"

Brilliant! The man is a genius, but unfortunately for them both, we were not letting the bicycle in the venue. After much discussion and funny remarks, he agreed his bicycle would have to stay outside.

"Will you keep an eye on him?" he asked. "I don't lock him up because he is a free spirit."

"Yeah, no problem. We'll keep an eye on him," replied Dave.

Into the venue walks our local celebrity. When I say walk, it's a cross between Max Wall and John Cleese! He went to the bar, ordered a pint and walked away with a roll-up cigarette drooping from his mouth. Now our celeb had a habit of talking to walls, which was hilarious to see, especially if punters didn't know who he was. They would just stare in amazement at him talking or arguing with a wall. This night, he started to argue with the wall. I don't know what the argument was about because I couldn't hear him because of the music, but I could tell by his actions. After much waving of his arms, he stood back from the wall, finished his pint, waved his hand one more time and walked to leave the pub. On the way out, he said to Dave and me in an angry voice, "I'm not being spoken to like that!" We just looked at each other and cracked up laughing even more. So, now our disgruntled Celeb has got the hump with the wall, he headed towards his bike and said, "C'mon, we're leaving." He went to mount his bike and fell off it. Me and Dave were now proper crying at what was going on in front of us. Our celeb gets back to his feet and starts shouting at his bike "Think you're fucking clever, do ya? Wait till I get you home. Don't think you'll be sleeping in the house tonight; you're going in the shed!"

People were walking up to the venue watching a man having a domestic argument with his bike and two doormen crying with laughter. Yeah, I know what you are thinking, not very professional of us, but I would defy anybody not to be lost in hysterics with what was going on right in front of us. Wait; it got better! So, eventually, our local Celeb mounted his bike and rode off with a bent, drooping, unlit rolled-up ciggie drooping from his mouth. It didn't matter that it was not lit, he's still sucking his cheeks in trying to get a puff of smoke. He travelled about 50 to 60 metres and arrived at another venue, dismounted from his bike and started talking to the doorman of that venue, obviously asking if him and the bike could come in. Now, judging by the bodily actions of all concerned, it wasn't happening, so eventually, our local Celeb mounted his bike and spun the front wheel around 90 degrees in preparation to ride off. As he did so, he smashed into a sandwich advertising board, taking himself, the bike and the board to the floor. Now we were struggling to stand up through laughing! As he got up, he lifted his bike in the air and started screaming, "Think you're hard, do you, cos you've got your mate with ya?" obviously referring to the sandwich board as being the bicycle's mate. "Fucking ganging up on me, are ya? Well, let's have it; I'll take ya both on!" The doormen of this other venue, on this occasion, happened to be more professional than me and Dave. They approached our Celeb and were trying to calm him down. I walked closer to the other venue so I could hear what was being said more clearly. One of the doormen was trying to explain that the sandwich board didn't mean anything personal by getting involved. Stone me! Now the doormen were believing that the board was a living creature! Our friend was growling and huffing and puffing, looking well angry at his bike and then at the sandwich board. "Fuck this shit, I'm off home. You can't even come out for a quiet night out without there being trouble," he said as he started to ride off on his bicycle. As he got further away from me, I could still hear him moaning at his bicycle. I always wondered if they made up that night and the bicycle ended up in the shed, or in the house with a good oiling down.

18.

Tribute Acts

One night, I was on the door at this venue and it was a Saturday night and they used to have on a tribute act every week. To be fair, I had only seen probably four bad acts in the six years I ran the door. We had all sorts of tribute acts there, from the old artists to the new artists. They were good nights, a bit like the old cabaret nights. I enjoyed them and enjoyed working them. They were always busy and it was nearly always a good night with no trouble. My favourite act by far was always the George Michael impersonator. The man was brilliant; he was funny, courteous and had an infectious personality. He was a flirt and he was so cheeeeeesey, he put the DAM in Edam. He was an ugly fucker but all he had to do was put on a wig, a pair of those light-shaded sunglasses and a police uniform and he was transformed into a global superstar singing in a village pub. He would sing George Michael songs and, of course, Wham songs. Now, everybody knows Wham lyrics and when they've had a few sherberts, they like to have a sing-along. He had the crowd going right from the start of his show! These nights were always packed to capacity, or fire limit, as they like to say nowadays in our world of political correctness. Loads of bored, cake-baking, chubby housewives used to turn up and get pissed and dance in front of the stage; in their drunken stupor, they probably thought they were in their teens again, single and slim. What I never got was the amount of them that used to have their pictures taken with the tribute acts at the end of the night. I mean, do me a fucking favour, love; 'TRIBUTE' - the clue is there right in front of ya! That did my nut in; weirdos.

Anyway, this one night, George Michael was on doing his usual crowd-entertaining show. The place was jumping, I mean, the whole place was dancing and singing, and I was loving it! The bored housewives were at the front of the stage, as usual, fluttering their eyelashes, and George was milking it, flirting back with them as he always did. He got to the interval in his act and told the crowd he would be back in half an hour. He slid away to the side of the stage and got chatting to one of the local housewives who was in there with her mates - probably on her once-a-month pass to come out - it was the only time I used to see her out. I knew this woman. I had seen her about when I was taking my kids to school and I knew a few people who knew her. She had always given off the aura of respectability, prim and proper; don't know about prim but she could definitely have made a Prop...a in rugby terms!

Next to the stage was a fire exit that led to the patio, that, in turn, led to the car park. Now, every Saturday night we would reserve a parking place near the fire door for the tribute act to park up so they could get their equipment in with no fuss; easy peasy. So, of course, some of the acts sometimes would take advantage of having their van outside the door and also take advantage of what was being put on offer, if you get my meaning.

George and our housewife tried very discreetly to slip out the fire exit without being noticed, but really, it was about as discreet as a fart in a sleeping bag. The other two lads on the door and myself clocked this and had a fairly good idea what was going to happen; there was going to be some father-figuring going on outside in a few minutes. So, we started giggling like little schoolkids planning our tactical manoeuvres to sneak up on the van and we set off outside, leaving the bar with no doormen. Fuck it, there wouldn't be any trouble, and if there was, we'd just tell the landlord we were dealing with an altercation outside.

The car park was set out like an L shape, so as we left one fire exit, you had to walk to the corner then turn left to get to the other fire exit where the tribute act would have their van parked. We slowly popped our heads around the corner and looked at the small white Peugeot van. We could see a bit of movement, not a lot, but obviously, something was going on in the van, so we quietly approached, holding in our silent laughter as we all looked at each other, then back to the van. As we got closer, the van rocked more, then closer, more rocking; it was like a synchronized Peeping Tom movement. Then we heard groans and moans - no, not the sort saying, "Have you cut the grass?"- those moans you hear in porno movies, so I've been told. That was it, it was obvious they were at it, a bit of the old tiffing, and then we heard it; the famous words that brought three doormen to their knees without one bit of violence being shown, threatened or given:

"Sing to me, George, sing to me, oh please, sing me a song!"

Well, we just collapsed to the floor laughing, but as were there on the floor, he started singing; out of tune a bit, but we could let him off with that due to the circumstances of the crowded van and exercise he was doing at that specific moment.

"Turn a different corner and we never would have met".

"Ooohhhh, sing it, sing it!" she blurted out. He carried on singing. We were crying, holding our sides; we were not so quiet now. As we started to withdraw from our peeping mission, I was hoping he would be withdrawing soon as he was due back on stage! They were none the wiser of us being there.

We entered back into the bar and as we did so, it seemed as if the whole place was looking at us, with our red cheeks, red tear-filled eyes and big daft smiles on our faces, so of course, people started asking what we'd been up to. "What's wrong? What's gone on?" Blah, blah, blah, fuck 'em; we weren't telling them or letting on. Most decent doormen wouldn't do that unless there was a personal vendetta against either the singer or the chubby, bored, cake-making, prim and propa housewife. Besides, sometimes I think ink can definitely be mightier than the sword. About a few minutes after we were back in the pub, George Michael bounced onto the stage with a big smug grin on his face and started shouting,

"Are we having a good time out there tonight?"

"Yeeeeeaaaahhhhhhh!!!!!!!!!!" roared back the crowd, and off he went, singing away and everybody started dancing again. Just as I started to wonder where the cake-maker was, she walked in the door I was stood next to. I looked at her and said, "Alright?"

She replied with a flustered rosy face, "Yeah, I needed some fresh air."

"Oh, really? You've been gone ages," I said back with a smug grin on my face. "You didn't get lost round the corner, did you? You should have taken a different one."

BOOM! She'd sussed me out and if looks could kill, I'd have been a goner right there and then! Never mind the two lads on the door with me laughing, giving the game away; she knew that I knew. She quickly walked past me and made her way through the crowd to her friends near the front of the stage, exchanged a few words and headed back towards where we were standing. She walked past us and straight out the door, never to be seen again, well, not by us on the door. Apparently, she's well known on Facebook for always going on about her cooking skills - yeah, I said the C-word and not the F-word.

19.

Mobility Fraud

One night, I was on the door at this venue; a nice place; a bit of a bar for locals. Some of them were up their own arse, you know, all that materialistic bollocks, but you used to get people coming from outside the area. The food was great, the entertainment was good and you knew it was always going to be busy. I used to visit this bar quite a lot myself when I was out for a drink. Now, amongst the locals was this couple I couldn't stand the sight of, for no other reason than they thought they were local celebs. He was about 5ft 6" and looked like one of the Super Mario brothers. He talked shit, bored everybody and he honestly thought he was God's gift to women and had slept with nearly all the women in town. How do I know that? Because he told me and the lads on the door on numerous occasions! You sussed it yet? Small man syndrome; Thumbelina was too tall for him. His partner, well, she worked down the Jobcentre and thought that everybody was beneath her; even businessmen who visited the bar she thought were below her (meaning she wanted to be on top). She was caught a couple of times bringing her own booze into the pub. One time, she was caught on the patio with a couple of bottles of wine in her bag. Every time she got barred, she would go see the gaffer of the pub and he would let her back in, much to the disgust of the doormen and bar staff. Eventually, I saw red about this and confronted the gaffer.

"Oi, why the fuck do you keep letting that bitch in every time she gets caught smuggling her own booze in? Nobody in here likes her or her old man, the fucking Hobbit wannabe."

I can't believe I didn't suss this out before, and this was his whispered reply;

"Leave it out, Matty, I've been giving her one now and then. Give her a bit of the old champers and she's well up for it. She can't afford to buy it, can she? So, I sort her out a bottle and she sorts me out."

I just broke out in a big smile, shook my head and called him a sneaky cunt. He started to laugh with me and told me not to say anything.

Yeah, right! I walked straight back to the lads I was working with and told them! They all started laughing and saying, "Nice one!" They didn't like Super Mario either, nobody did, but now when he used to come in the bar spouting off giving it large, instead of letting the plumber-faced twat annoy us, we would just laugh because we knew something he didn't, and that was his missus had been up the old wooden hill once she had necked her free champagne, and that wasn't the only thing she was necking on those nights!

Now, this one time on a Saturday night, the booze-smuggling dole worker showed up on a mobility scooter at the venue we were working. I didn't know what was up with her, wasn't bothered, to be honest. I thought it was just some new way for her to smuggle her own booze in again. She drove up to the door and parked up, gave me and the lads a 'you are shit on my shoes' look, and walked in.

"I fucking hate her and her old man," said one of the lads. "The bitch works down the dole centre and thinks she's better than everybody."

"Don't let 'em bother ya; tell her old man that the whole pub knows she's been shagging the gaffer; that'll piss them both off!"

Now here's what really fucking bugged me about the dole centre worker - she was going round telling everybody in this bar that she got the mobility scooter through the dole, on the sick, and because she knew the system, once she could walk again and was back at work, she was going to sell the mobility scooter for a nice little earner. This was the same woman who looked down her nose at all people, whether they be rich or poor, working or not, gay or straight, black or white, lager or champagne drinker. She didn't discriminate; she put the nob in snob, the mug in smuggler and the LICE in SLICE! Well, that's what the boss of the venue told us when he had to go down the clinic for the special shampoo you use in your downstairs department.

It got better! So, we were on the door keeping an eye on the place, as you do, the music was playing and everyone was having a good night. A few people were dancing as they do; the night cracked on, a few more people dancing, then, out of nowhere, up got the Dole Queen and started dancing, proper dancing. I looked at one of the lads and he looked at me and said, "Is she taking the fucking piss or what?"

There was obviously nothing wrong with her! She was fiddling the benefits system! The night went on and she carried on dancing, laughing and dancing. I had to walk out of the venue and get some fresh air as I had the right hump about her.

While I was stood outside, three lads who I knew from the area where I grew up came outside the venue, started chatting to me about bits and bobs, and then one of them comes out with;

"See that bitch in there that works down the dole centre dancing like a fucking demented ferret? Bitch got my benefits stopped for no fucking reason!"

"Yeah, I see her. I can't believe she's stood up dancing. She's on the sick; she had to get here on that mobility scooter," I replied, pointing to the mobility scooter,

"Anyway, lads, have a good night whatever you get up to. Take care; I'm off back inside," I said as I shook their hands and walked back into the venue.

The end of the night came, and people started leaving. It had been a good night and busy. As the crowd started to dwindle, I clocked the Dole Queen sat there all sweaty from her night's dancing and her plumber-faced fellow slumped over a chair, obviously the worse for wear. Just about every week we had this scenario with these 2 plastic local celebs. They wouldn't want to leave, always got mouthy, coming out with loads of sarcastic remarks; he would grow beer muscles, but we stayed professional in our work.

Last drinks served was at midnight. We would wait until about 12.15 and start shouting, "Start seeing your drinks off now, please," about every 2 minutes, then increase the number of shouts at around 12.25 and we would usually have the bar cleared for 12.30. Sometimes, if there were nice people left in, we would give them longer to drink up, or, if they had ordered a taxi and it was raining outside, we would just let them stay in the bar until the taxi arrived.

Now, the Dole Queen and the plumber-face thought they could do what they want. I think she thought that because she had shagged the gaffer of the bar a few times and he did because he was just a cunt. But tonight, our Super Mario could hardly walk.

"It's okay, it's okay, you can drive the mobility scooter and I'll walk," said the Dole Queen. As they walked out of the door, we heard her screaming, "What has gone on? Look what they've done! Who would do such a thing?" We walked outside not knowing what to expect, but as we got outside, we just cracked up laughing! Immediately outside the entrance were a couple of trees next to the car park, and the Dole Queen's mobility scooter was only placed up the tree wedged in between some branches! Fuck me, the Dole Queen only climbed the tree like a monkey and started trying to pull the scooter down!

"I'm off," I said to the lads. "Leave her to it; don't want anything to do with it."

The next day, I got a phone call from the gaffer of the bar.

"Do you know anything about that scooter being in the tree last night?" he asked me.

"No! Do I fuck; why?"

"Because the police are coming to see me. I've got CCTV of three lads lifting the mobility scooter onto the back of a pickup truck, then pulling up beside the tree and placing it there between some branches. She fell out the tree and has done her leg in. Apparently, she's going to need that mobility scooter now, in a genuine way."

I knew straight away which three lads he was on about, the ones from where I grew up. "Listen, erase the CCTV images and

I'll erase my memory of telling Super Mario you boned his missus for a swig of smuggled champagne."

He replied, "What CCTV?"

I replied, "What champagne?"

20.

Wet Gangster

One night on the door, I was working this venue and it was Christmas time, silly season, as we who work in the pub game like to call it. Your once-a-year drinkers; you know the sort, hide behind their curtains every night all year watching soaps on the TV, believing that Dirty Den is having an affair with Dot Cotton and that Coronation Street has a boozer where nobody ever goes to the toilet for a piss, shit or a cheeky line.

So, this one Friday night, we were getting ready for closing time. The DJ had played his last few songs for the erection section end of the night, the bit where all the people out on a works' night out start copping off with each other, then when they're back at work they can blame it on the alcohol because they are not normally like that the rest of the year. But tonight was their night to live the life of one of those soap stars off the box they have been watching all year.

"Start seeing your drinks off now, please, folks," I shouted as loud as I could as I was walking through the bar. Then, I started approaching groups of people and asking them politely,

"Start seeing your drinks off, please, folks."

Now, I know while I am doing this, the other doormen I am working with will be doing pretty much the same. I always found people responded better to being spoken to politely to drink up. Sometimes, in a group, you would get someone who was anti and couldn't handle their alcohol and would give you a bit of abuse back, and sure enough, tonight I had got myself one. Standing at the bar were two women and a man who I had asked a few times, very politely, to drink up. Every time I did so, the two women were polite and said they would be doing so, but the man always muttered something as I walked away. To be honest, I think the two women could have finished their drinks well before they did, but they felt obliged to babysit their argumentative friend. I mean this guy looked like a cross between Danny DeVito and Ronnie Corbett! He had the figure of an office worker, but the booze probably made him think he was 'Conan The Librarian'.

Now, you see, I'm not a bully - never have been - I hate bullies. I was bullied as a kid, physically and mentally, that's probably why I'm not right in the head, but I had a good reputation on the door for not being a bully, so no matter what my little stumpy friend gave me in abuse, I was never going to get physical with him. However, at the same time, you can't seem to look a mug on the door, so you have to sometimes get a bit verbal with people; I would say belittle him but he was already little.

So, after about three or four times of asking him to leave, he eventually made his way to the door, but as he did so, he was giving me a glare with his eyes that would frighten Mike Tyson, and he'd developed a swagger. He then asked me if I knew so and so, this person, that person, this gangster, that gangster, this hard man, that hard man, this family, that family. Fuck me, I thought I was in a quiz show! Some of them I knew, some I knew of and some, I think, were out of the movies. Anyway, he proceeded to tell me how he knew them all and that he was their very good friend. I mean, this librarian had more connections than getting the tube across London! The thing was, I'd heard it all before on numerous occasions, so I just smiled and humoured him; anything just to get him to fuck off.

But then, he came out with the cardinal sin of making threats towards my family. Every fucking doorman I knew hated that and if you were a punter, by doing that, you crossed the line, but what could I do? I didn't want to get physical with him. Eventually, we shut the door to the night club and we heard him making his way down the three flights of stairs. I walked behind the bar to help myself to a well-earned drink. Just as I was popping the top off my bottle of lager, I noticed one of the very large bottle tubs beside me, which was empty. Now, a bottle tub is just short in length of your average household bathtub but about 3ft deep, and they are on wheels, so I quickly rolled the tub under the nearest tap and started to fill the tub with water. I ran to the fire exit and opened the door and looked down to where people always stood waiting for a taxi, and there was my prey, stood on his own, swaying in the breeze! I went back into the club and returned to my bottle tub, which had about a foot and a half of water in it. I turned the tap off and rolled the tub towards the exit door and out onto the fire exit. Now, I couldn't lift the tub on my own over the 4ft handrail that went round the fire exit, so I called one of the doormen to give me hand to lift it. As we started lifting it, we got the giggles, so two of the DJs came out to see what we were up to. Just as we were about to release the tsunami of water on our friendly neighbourhood gangster, I looked down and shouted,

"Oi! Mate!" Haha, sure enough, he looked up and 'BADDDOOOSSSSHHHHHH' he got soaked with the contents of my water tub. We all quickly ran back inside the club absolutely crying out with laughter. I lost it big time! We could hear the thudding of steps running up the metal stairs of the fire exit and we knew it was him.

"Quick! Get rid of the tub!" I said to my fellow soakers.

Next came the thunderous banging on the fire exit door.

"Who is it?" I shouted at the fire doors so whoever was on the other side could hear me, knowing full well it was the wet gangster.

"Open the fucking door!" came the reply.

"Who is it?" I shouted again to the fire door.

Once more came the reply, "Open the fucking door!"

So, I composed myself and opened the fire exit to be greeted by a furious wet drip, puffing and panting. I reached my hands out to either side of me with my palms turned up and at the same time asked, "Has it been raining?"

The drip replied in a very angry snarling damp voice, "You're a fucking dead man! I know people. I'm gonna have you fucking shot!"

All innocently and angelic, I replied "Why you having me shot, mate? It's not my fault you didn't bring out an umbrella! Anyway, ya better get yasen off before ya catch ya death of cold." I took a step back and reached my hands out to either side of me, grabbing both the fire exit doors to pull them shut, to the sounds of my wet friend issuing more death threats to me and my family from all his gangster friends. As I went back behind the bar to get my bottle of lager, I was greeted by the two DJs pulling the bottle tub and the other doorman pushing it, and this time there were no half measures; the tub was proper full. We repeated the same scenario of getting it through the fire exit doors and onto the fire escape, but this time it was a lot heavier so it was going to take all four of us to lift it up and tip it over the handrail.

One of the DJs said, "Get ready, after 3, 1, 2, 3!" as we lifted and tipped in the one smooth motion! I looked down and shouted "Oi!" Fuck me, he only looked up again as the second tsunami of water smashed into him! Myself and the three soakers quickly ran back into the club and shut the fire exit. On doing so, we lost it; we were all in fits of hysterics! We could hear the thunderous footsteps coming up the stairs, but at the same time, the owner of the club had appeared from doing his cashing up, and so had the other bar staff and doormen. The owner of the club looked at us and just started laughing; he didn't even know what we were laughing at, which sets us off with even more laughing. Then the bar staff all start laughing at us laughing and the owner started laughing which set off the other doormen laughing! By now, the wet gangster started banging on the fire exit door, screaming,

"Open the fucking door, ya cunts, open the fucking door!!!!"

This just increased the laughing amongst us! Now, there was no way the four of us who did the water crime were going to open the door, so the owner of the club went to the fire exit doors, and opened them to be greeted by the wet gangster, absolutely soaking. Well, that was it. He lost it and eventually blurted out, "Who the fuck are you?" then just bent over in hysterics. Everybody else's laughter increased at the sight of the wet gangster, who then started shouting threats at the owner, the bar staff and the other doormen, but every time he shouted out, it increased the laughter pains in us all. The owner of the club still had no idea who he was or how he had got wet! When he finally composed himself, he asked him, "Has it been raining?" but he wasn't being sarcastic - he genuinely didn't know because he had been stuck in the back cashing up the night's takings.

"No, it hasn't been fucking raining!" replied the wet gangster. "Some cunt has thrown a bucket of water over me!" The owner cracked up again and said, "Fuck me, that's some size bucket! I wouldn't like to carry that up and down a hill!" We all just increased the laughter pains. This wet gangster was looking at us thinking, 'What the fuck is going on with these nutters? They are fucking mental!' I think the water had sobered him up as well. He turned to walk down the fire escape but just before he went, he shouted out one gurgle of threats, the usual bollocks, that he was coming back with his mates next week and that we were all dead. The owner of the club shouted after him,

"You fucking bring who ya want, mate! We'll be ready and waiting. I'm going out tomorrow to buy some water pistols, and if ya want to get proper heavy, I'll buy my boys a couple of garden hoses with different settings!" As he finished shouting this, we were dripping tears of laughter; the tears could have filled another bottle tub.

The following weekend, we all turned up for work and were stood on the door chatting about this and that, and up popped the owner of the club with a cheap plastic water pistol in each hand. For a short while after, I used to wonder about the wet gangster, wonder if he was telling stories to other people about how he beat up four doormen at a nightclub and that he got drenched in their blood and not in water! Wonder if he was reading loads more criminal books while working as Conan The Librarian. In all my years of working the door, he wasn't the first who carried on like that and he was definitely not the last.

21.

Twisted Firestarter

One night on the door, I was working this club; it was a rave club with two floors. Downstairs had the old-style piano garage music playing, and upstairs was jungle music which was just coming onto the music scene. To be honest with ya, even though I was only probably about 22 at the time, I fucking hated the constant boom, boom, fucking boom of the jungle music! I preferred the garage music; still do, probably because of the good and sometimes nearly bad memories it brings to me. Anyway, so this club was alright to work. We had our fair share of trouble, had a huge drugs problem that went with that sort of music, and on the door, you were fighting a losing battle trying to control/ban it; it was gurn central. But the club was out the way of all the other main nightlife in the two towns either side of us. What made it so popular was the DJ/MCs/Grooveriders; don't know what the fuck they were calling them back then. They all had different names. What made the club so popular was that the couple that owned it used to bring in all the top names at that time, whether it be DJs or dance acts. Also, the other bonus they had was they had a great host DJ/MC, best I ever worked with. We worked a lot together at different venues and clubs over the years. He did well for himself and commanded a lot of money and people paid it. (Respect, Mr Baker).

So, this one particular night, the management had hired this dance act to show up. Word spread around town, obviously. Now we, the doormen, knew we were going to be full to the rafters, and the management knew it as well, but they had paid a lot of money to secure this act, a lot of added bonuses for them to come and perform. You know what I mean - part of the money through the books and part of it in cash - hotels and added expenses all paid for.

I remember this one time they paid a world-famous DJ £800 cash to call in as he was on his way from one venue to another. Fuck me, £800 cash for half an hour! This was in 1992, but the management were very shrewd and they knew all they had to do was advertise him being there on the night and the place would be full. As long as a few people got to see him they wouldn't give a fuck that he was only on for half an hour; the rest of the night they would be monged out their heads.

So, the night of the dance act coming to the venue arrived. Me and the other lads usually started at 9, but this night we started a bit earlier. When we arrived, the queue was halfway around the block, four wide.

"For fuck sake, that queue alone is going to fill the club. We're going to be well over our fire limit. We got extra lads on tonight?" I said to the head doorman.

"Nope, just the usual six," he replied all casual. Now, let me tell you, six was never enough to run this club on any normal night, a club with 2 floors, with nooks and crannies all over the place. It's no wonder it had a drug problem (yeah, they couldn't get enough).

So, we opened the doors and started letting in the punters, doing our usual drug searches (waste of time) half of them walking through the door were already in gurn fest mode, fucking mouths all over the place slobbering like a boxer dog with a wobbly jaw. The place was filled up within about half an hour of opening the doors; it was like being in the Christmas sales! I looked at the head doorman and gaffer of the venue,

"Are we still going to keep letting people in?" I asked them both.

And with a big cheesy greedy smile on his face, the gaffer of the venue just nodded his head forward, meaning yes.

At about 10 pm, a customised transit van pulled up at the front of the venue. It was obvious to me and everybody stood there at that time that this would be the dance act. I thought there would have been some kind of arrangement for them to arrive down a side entrance or around the back. The side door of the van slid open and out got the four lads, no minders, bodyguards or security, just a driver with them, and they started making their way up the stairs and to the main door.

"Quick, Matty, get them upstairs out the way into the back room!" shouted the head doorman. I put out my hands like an aeroplane and started walking sidewards like a drunken crab, forcing myself through the crowd with my leading hand, and letting my trailing hand be a sort of guide for the dance act to follow me. We reached the safety of the back room and I shut the door to all the chaos and booming dance music out in the main club area. The first thing that struck me about these lads was how humble they were; you could just tell by meeting them they were good lads. The second thing that struck me was the smell of the funny cigarette they were smoking.

The door burst open and in walked the gaffer, big smile on his face. He reached out his hand towards one of the dance act who was smoking the old Jamaican Woodbine.

"Alright, lads, safe journey? Did you get here okay? Anything you need? Any problems, just ask Matty; he'll sort them for you."

They were just lounging about on old chairs and carpets looking at him, showing no emotion; I don't think they could be arsed with him, to be honest. The gaffer left the room, and they just started talking amongst themselves. Then I heard the word snowboarding. I liked to do a bit of snowboarding myself at that time.

"'Ere, I do a bit of snowboarding," I threw into the mix of their conversation.

"Oh really? Nice one! Where you done that at?" asked one of the tall members of the act.

That's it now; I'm crashed out with them chatting about snowboarding like I've known them years. They're passing around their cigarette, laughing and joking, or should I say 'laughing and toking'. In all my years of working the doors, the most laid back I had ever seen any act that was about to perform. Then I started wondering where were all the bags and outfits and other sorts of props usually associated with artists that were going to be performing, so I asked them that exact question. They all started laughing.

"The driver sets it all up - we just dance, do a bit of EmCeeing and go on stage as we are, and pop one of these," said one of the act, pulling a little bag of tablets out of his pocket. Now, as he did this, one of the barmaids entered the room with some cold bottles of water they had requested. As soon as she walked in, she pulled a face at the smell in the room from the funny cigarettes, then she clocked the bag of pills the act member was holding.

"Ohhhh nooo, no drugs in this place!" she shouted out. "I'm ringing the police and you lot had better leave! We're not having any of that carry on in these premises!" I couldn't believe what I was hearing; for a second, I thought she was joking, then I realised the silly cow was being serious. I jumped to my feet and grabbed her arm and semi-dragged her to the door, then whispered a shout at her, you know what I mean? You're trying to whisper but your emotions are making you shout?

"Are you for fucking real? You work in a rave club, and you're saying you don't agree with drugs? That's like working in a church and saying you don't believe in God, ya dizzy motherfucker! If these guys leave without performing, all them pill-heads out there will fucking riot, now fuck off out of here and send the gaffer to see me!" I turned to the lads and started to apologise. I don't think any of what happened just registered with them, so they didn't know what the fuck I was apologising for; I don't even think they knew where they were by then.

The gaffer didn't show up to the room - he probably couldn't make his way through the crowds, or he was doing his usual 'out the rear fire exit getting a nosh off a bird' routine. The dance act went on stage and gave a fantastic performance, not long but quality. I found it funny watching from the side of the stage, all these young people trying to dance in a room more crammed than a tin of sardines. It was good though, the dance act came over well, had a good rapport with the crowd, and I can tell you that's how they were off stage, a genuine good bunch of lads.

When we got back to the room, the sweat coming of these lads was in bucketloads and the steam from their bodies was just like walking into a sauna. Now, the door went again and in walked their driver with a couple of holdalls, which, when they unzipped them, held a change of clothes and some towels.

As they are getting changed, the gaffer walked into the room with a big smile.

"Thanks, lads, that was amazing, top night." He then looked at me. "What went on earlier with that dizzy cow, the barmaid?" I half-turned my back on the dance act getting stripped off and changing, well, I didn't want to look like a pervert or something like that, and explained to him what had gone on. He then went on to explain to me that she had come down ranting and raving about the goings-on in the room and that I was partying with the act.

"Fucking partying? I was sat chatting to them about snowboarding and other things, the lying cow!" I shouted in one of my whispers. As I was saying this, it must have caught the attention of the act because they all start looking in my direction.

"You okay, Matty?" one of them asked. I didn't even think they knew my name!

"Yeah, I'm okay," I replied, "just a bit of bollocks with that barmaid earlier on, stupid cow, be lucky I don't set her car alight!"

"No need, Matty, let it go, chill, don't get all twisted over it, no need to go starting fires, just relax and don't be that twisted fire starter," he said to me as he cracked up another Jamaican Woodbine. And do you know? He was right! I didn't go and be a twisted fire-starter, but he did.

22.

Millwall

One night on the door, I was working this boozer, and the gaffer came out and told me he had just bought this hotel and its local. Only thing was, when the local team played at home, the two bars they had in the hotel were the bars recommended by the police for the travelling away fans, so he needed to put some kind of security on. Could I sort it out?

"Yeah, no probs," I replied. He cleared off and my doorman partner who was working with me looked at me, started laughing and said,

"Fuck me, you'll need some boy to work that, won't ya?"

"No, will I fuck, we'll do it with two of us and charge more. Fucking easy!"

He looked at me like I was a diddler fiddler, high on my own supply. So, I started to explain it to him. "It's like this; I've worked a few football matches, always for the home fans, one maybe two locked doors round the back of the venue or maybe one locked door at the front, then if any away fans turn up, you're always nice and tell them it's a 'home fans' pub' then tell them where the away fans' pubs are. Easy. If you get a load of aggro boys turn up, you just do the same. They are not going to kick off with you because usually, they have the police following them." (You have got to remember this was the 90s; BIG BROTHER was watching.) "You might get the odd group of lads who break away from the Old Bill; just don't open the doors for them or you baffle them with bullshit over brains and just tell them that you have police in the premises dealing with something, give them a wink and a nod and some sound advice about not getting nicked."

"Yeah, yeah, yeah, fucking great that, Matty, but that's home fans' pubs you've worked. What about fucking working the away fans? They'll fucking skin us alive, you fucking idiot!" my partner told me with a mixture of anger and anxiety. My partner was no div; he had the nickname of 'Scally'. I never knew why that was his nickname, never asked; come to think of it, I still don't know why that was his nickname. He was the furthest you're ever likely to get from a Scallywag! He was a kind caring lad, good-looking fucker as well, but on the flip side, he was fucking hard as nails. ABA boxing champ when he was younger, we used to train in the same boxing gym; he was fit as fuck. This lad would be able to cycle John O' Groats to Land's End in a couple of days, not just on any cycle, but a unicycle, and he was that fit he would do it on a unicycle with a flat tyre... with a backpack on.

Anyway, I said to my young protégé, "Calm the fuck down. I've seen that hotel when its full of away fans. It always has the police parked outside; you don' really need doormen, it fucking runs itself. Besides, if there is any trouble, we'll just fuck off; there is nothing a few doormen can do against two bars full of away fans; this ain't fucking Roadhouse!"

What I didn't realise was the gaffer was hiring the old manageress of the hotel to run things for a while, so she put him straight about not always needing doormen for away games because of the police being outside, and that they were mainly there to stop the home fans from kicking off. So, he

127

didn't need us for a couple of weeks. The first time he needed us was for a game against a Millwall.

I received a phone call during the week at work from the owner of the hotel;

"How you doing, Matthew? Will I be seeing you on Friday night at my bar as usual?"

Before I could reply, he went on to say, "I've been talking with the manageress and we've decided we could do with some security on Saturday."

I thought to myself 'Yeah, no fucking shit, Sherlock! Ring the MOD; see if there's a regiment free this weekend!'

"Will you be able to sort it, Matthew? I'll leave a kitty for you and your lads and you pay accordingly to the numbers of security you will require."

"Okay, cheers," I replied, hoping that I would be needed that weekend in my daytime job so I could give it a swerve. I rang Scally and told him the script about what was happening and told him what I was planning, so he agreed to go along with it and reminded me it would be his first time working a football match.

"Don't worry about it, it will be fine!" I told him as I rolled the eyes into the back of my head and looked to the sky for some kind of sign from God.

Saturday morning arrived and we got to the hotel for 11 am in time for the bar opening. As usual, there was a police van and a police car parked outside. I knew some of the police in the van; two of them were okay, two of them were not in my dealings, and I didn't know the rest of them. As the morning turned into early afternoon, more and more Millwall fans were starting to arrive at the hotel and go into the main bar. There was a bit of a patio area at the back of the main bar with a gate leading back onto the front of the hotel where we were stood and the police were parked. Part of our job was to keep checking the gate and make sure it was closed. The day was going okay; we were chatting with some of the fans and having a bit of banter, and they were quite happily necking the beers and, to be honest, they were mainly families, you know what I mean, fans. I've worked a lot of football matches in different capacities, venues, events, football grounds, bars, clubs. I've seen the best and the worse of most teams. I'd worked Millwall football matches at bars in previous years but this day just seemed to be more relaxed, or so I thought.

Now, it was getting to about half an hour before kick-off and the noise from the bars was getting louder and the songs they were singing were just blending into one. I wished for a time machine to just hurry up the next half hour, to get them out of the hotel and to the ground, then it was not our problem. You'll never guess what happened next! The police in the van started their engine, the bobby in the passenger side leant out of the wound-down window and shouted,

"Have fun, boys, we're out of here!"

And they drove off, with a van full of laughing policeman. I couldn't believe it; them being there was a bit of a deterrent stopping both sets of fans getting out of line! I turned to Scally to say something and he was not there. Now my heart was proper pumping. 'Awww, fuck me, where's he gone?' I thought to myself. It was obvious he'd walked into the bar, so I spun on the spot, went into the hotel just catching him as he was about to enter one of the bars.

"What the fuck you doing"? I asked him, grabbing his arm.

"I was just going to ask them to keep the singing down a bit," he replied. I nearly fainted!

"Are you fucking real? If they want to sing, let them! Working the footy is different to working other times in clubs and bars, oh and the police have fucked off!" and with that, he nearly fainted. In a matter of moments, we became the faint brothers!

I said, "Look, if it goes off, we'll just fucking go off, off somewhere else, fuck staying around if it kicks off. We've got a kitty to spend, and we don't want to be spending it in hospital on fucking Werther's Originals!" He nodded his head in agreement with me.

Time went on and the Millwall fans started leaving the hotel to get to the game for the 3 pm kick-off, probably stopping off at the chip shop on the way. As they were leaving, we had a bit of friendly banter with them and everything was going okay, thank the lord. I looked at Scally and said,

"That's got to be it; the bar must be nearly empty by now. I'll go check."

I walked into the bar and there were two lads left. One of them was at the bar arguing with the barmaid about a missing pint; the barmaid was about 5ft 4". When I say these ", I should have said, this geezer and this lad, because the one at the bar was a proper geezer. He turned round, looked at me and growled, "Alright, mate, how's it going?" His eyes were just like a shark's eyes, black and lifeless. He had teeth like a smashed-up graveyard and a couple of scars on his face just to complete the imitation factor. I thought to myself, 'This bloke is like 'THE THING' out of the Fantastic Four, but bigger, harder and scarier.'

I took a deep breath, on the sly of course; like dogs, a proper geezer will sense fear.

"What's up, mate? Can I help?" I asked.

"Yeah, some cunt has nicked my pint!"

'Fuck me,' I thought, 'he's at it'. I leant over the bar and told the barmaid to get him, his mate, me and Scally a pint, then pull the railings down and shut the bar. Feeling smug, I was thinking that was a nasty confrontation avoided; him and his mate get a free pint, I get to keep my limbs intact, the bar shuts so they'll leave without even making a big deal about it. Well, that's what I thought.

"No!" shouted back the little aggressive barmaid. "You and Scally can have a pint, but them two fuckers ain't!"

I looked at the geezer and smiled then leant back over the bar and told her, "It's okay, I'll clear it with the owner, just pour the beers!"

"No!!!!" she shouted once more. Now, I have a choice - I can either piss off the barmaid who looks like an extra from any Hobbit film, or I can piss off the Millwall geezer who looks like an extra from any giant film; fucking no brainer. I leant over the bar and summoned the barmaid over, leant as far as I could over the bar and put my mouth just to the side of her face and whispered something that made a big smile appear on her face, and off she went to pour the lagers.

"Fakin' 'ell sun, dunno what ya said there but it fakin' worked!" growled the geezer. We all started to drink our lagers and Scally asked,

"How the fuck did you get her to pour the lagers?" Before replying, I made sure the barmaid was out of earshot and then proceeded to tell them.

"I told her I would let you take her upstairs in one of the hotel rooms and fuck her." As I finished telling them, Scally spat out a mouthful of beer and the two Millwall fans cracked up laughing. We started getting a good yarn on with the two fans and they were telling us they hadn't even got tickets for the match. It was a spur of the moment idea to travel up to the match and now they weren't even interested in going to the game.

"Four more lagers?" shouted the barmaid, unexpectedly, from behind the bar as she had already started pouring the first pint.

"Yeah, go on then, why not?" I shouted back and then immediately turned to Scally and whispered, "She's trying to get you pissed so she can have her wicked way with you!" We all started to laugh again, apart from Scally.

Scally and myself carried on talking with the two Millwall lads about everything from football to the North/South divide, to jobs prospects in our respective areas, and as we got near the end of our lagers, the barmaid started to pour some more for us. Scally leant forward a bit and whispered "I'm gonna have to slide off. I'm not letting you pimp me out to a hobbit! In a minute I'll make out I'm off to the toilet and do one."

Five minutes later he was gone. Five minutes after that the barmaid has sussed out what's gone on and she's not a happy hobbit;

"Well, somebody better take me upstairs and sort me out before I go!!" she shouted from behind the bar. Before I could reply, the big geezer volunteered.

"Right, let's go upstairs then, I've got a room sorted. Matty, you watch the bar."

I'm thinking to myself, 'I don't fucking believe this', but I looked at the other Millwall lad and said, "Fancy another lager?"

Roughly twenty minutes later, the lovebirds appeared back in the room with big smug smiles upon their faces. The big rough hard-as-fuck Millwall geezer looked at me and said, "I fakin' love this town".

I left the bar with the two geezers in there having their own little private party with the barmaid. Funny how things can turn around; that barmaid hated the two of them, the Old Bill were shit scared of all the fans in the bars in the hotel, and everybody was just expecting a day of aggro and it turned to be a day of love.

FUNNY OLD GAME, this door malarkey.

23.

Snowball Fights with Other Doormen

One night on the door and I was working this venue that has had really good Christmas and New Year takings, same as all the other bars on the strip. It was January, and as usual in the pub game, January and February are always fairly quiet months. You usually find that the owners of bars, pubs, clubs and venues will be nowhere to be seen in these months, stashing their cash sales abroad somewhere, all holidaying in the sun, or just taking a bit of time off. I don't blame them, to be honest, plus, it's nice to have a few quiet nights with no gaffer overlooking your every move, especially after all the hassle and stress over Christmas.

So, me and my partner were stood outside wrapped up in more clothes than an arctic expedition, constantly moving about to keep warm, nipping inside the venue to get heat in our bodies, drinking hot tea and talking the usual shit about the past week's events and what we've been up to. It was an easy night to work but it was just so fucking boring and the night dragged like the arse of a dog with no legs. With every breath, a big puff of cold smoke exhaled from our lungs. The roads had heaps of piled-up slush and snow at the side of them from the days of snow we had been having, while the middle of the roads had a layer of fresh snow that had been falling that evening. It was fucking miserable; the weather was miserable, the pubs were dead, the only people that were out were walking about miserable, mostly because they were dressed like it was summer and it was winter. So, you had to occupy your mind with something if the barmaids, or barmen for that matter, didn't want to nip off to the toilet for a bit of the old 'how's ya father'.

This night, as we were stood on the door, a snowball came whizzing past mine and my partner's heads, and as we looked to each other waiting for one of us to explain what the fuck was going on, another two snowballs whizzed past and hit the bar window! We both turned towards the direction they came from, which was a car park that backed on to a popular bar across the road. We both ran over to catch the culprits, but nobody was there. We could only see the back doors of the hotel bar lit up in the fresh falling snow. Two doormen who we both knew were stood there. They worked for one of the local doorman agencies in the area, probably the biggest, and they had all the bars surrounding the bar I was running at the time. We shouted over to the two doormen;

"Oi! You seen any kids about lobbing snowballs?"

"No," they replied. My partner and I looked at each other, both thinking the same thing; well, they must be around here somewhere.

We walked back to our door and whoosh, fuck me, a load of snowballs came whizzing past my head. I spun round to the direction I had just walked from, but again, nobody was there. I put my leg down ready to start to sprint and slipped on the snow. My partner started laughing at me as I was laid on the floor soaking wet, cold and not very happy.

"Quick, ya useless cunt, get over there and see where the fuck they are!" I shouted out to my partner in an 'I'm blaming you' voice.

He ran off across the road to the car park. The cunt must have had his non-slip shoes on because as much as I had his back and he had mine, I was dying to see him slip and go over into the slushy icy snow. As I was getting back to my feet, from my left, two doormen walked up from one of the other bars in the area, smiling.

"What the fuck is going on here, then?" they asked me, all smug,

"You been done over, or slipped?"

"Fucking slipped; fucking kids keep throwing snowballs at us. If I catch 'em I'm going into Elf mode!" (if you've ever seen the film Elf with Will Ferrell, you'll know what I'm talking about). With that, my partner came back from the car park across the road, shrugged his shoulders and told me,

"Nope, they've gone again."

At the same time, one of our two inquisitive doormen spoke into his radio.

"Yeah, received and understood, can't really speak now."

We couldn't hear what was being said because he had one of these earphones in his ear, you know the ones I mean - the police wear them and doormen wear them because they're all fucking Kevin Costner wannabes. The doorman who had been speaking into his radio said,

"Okay, see ya later. We better get back to our bar. We're dead as well which makes it a long night. It's boring, isn't it? Have a good night!"

Waffle, waffle, fucking waffle! Now, his pleasantries as he was walking away set alarm bells ringing in my head. My partner looked at me and said,

"What the fuck is that about? 'I can't really speak right now'. We all know each other!" As soon as he'd said these words, we both twigged what was going on. The message he received would have been from the other doormen at the back of the hotel bar. It was them throwing the snowballs! They were all part of the same doorman agency, that's why these other two doormen showed up, probably having a laugh at me slipping on the snow.

Now, we were game on, all systems were go! It was a shit night so now we were going to liven it up, with some war games or thaw games. I know some of you will be reading this thinking I've heard about doorman wars before, guns and knives and who controls the drugs, well, this doorman war was different. Like I already said numerous times before, I wasn't a gangster or into any of that gangster shit; it meant being a bully and nasty which is not in my nature, and I can't be like that. This doorman war was a snowball war. And if we were going to get nasty, we might use some iceballs; that's about as gangster as I got.

Me and my partner started planning; we were going to be out-numbered, and there were going to be snowballs raining down on us from all over once it went over the radio to the other agency doormen. We both looked at each other, grinning, and gave a leather-gloved high 5. It felt like a scene out of the Goonies, only older, balder and probably a lot more immature.

The first plan of attack was on the hotel bar doormen, as we were opposite them, then, on the way back, the club to our left would be their doorman on the counter-attack, probably followed by the bar to our right. We didn't need Kevlar vests that night - we needed Kevlar balaclavas!

We started making our supply of snowballs, keeping a lookout for any sniper fire. Two of the regulars came out of the bar, both of them roughly in their 30s, and asked us what we were doing. I explained what had been going on while rounding off another snowball in my black leather gloves.

One of them flicked his cigarette away and said, "I'll have some of that; it's fucking boring out tonight!" I thought to myself, 'Nice one, we've got two mercenaries on board.'

We had a heap of snowballs by the door, a few in my hands and two in each pocket of my Crombie overcoat. "Right, let's do this!" I said to my battalion. We ran across the road into the hotel car park and took the two doormen on the back door by surprise; quality ambush! They started ducking for cover as they opened the door to get inside.

"We done 'em! Let's head back to base!" I shouted out, half out of breath, half laughing.

Sure enough, as we crossed the road to get back to our bar, the club from the left had their doorman firing snowballs at us. The hotel doormen had got on the radio to them, and at the same time, from the bar to our right, we could see their doormen advancing a few steps at a time, then bending down to gather snow to make balls. It was a proper life or death scenario now - to make it back to the heap of snowballs we had left outside the bar or we were done for. We made it back to our heap of snowballs and tried to fire back at our enemies, but we were outnumbered and the snowballs were smashing into us, into the door and into the bar window. We retreated behind the door for cover and warmth to the thudding sound of snowballs hitting the windows and doors. The bar manager came storming over to us as we stood there brushing the snow off ourselves, in fits of giggles, and shouted at us, "What the fuck is going on?" I never liked him so I grabbed his arm as I opened the door with my other hand and pulled him to the door before pushing him outside and watching him getting battered by the onslaught of snowballs! I thought he was going to start crying! Best way to describe the way he looked as the snowballs stopped raining in - like a scene out of Bugsy Malone after a splurge gun fight.

So, we turned a boring January night into something a little more exciting, but it doesn't end there. So, if the pub trade is slow in January, obviously, there is nothing for our local constabulary to do. About ten minutes after all this had ended, up pulled a riot van outside our bar, followed by a police car, and out of the van stepped one of the local bobbies who, to be fair, was old school and in all of my dealings with him he was fair; hard, but fair. He walked up to me and my door partner, stopped and stood at ease, then squatted his frame and said with a big cheeky grin,

"Evening all, what's been happening round here then? We've had a report of an assault on your bar manager!" My partner and myself started laughing, thinking he was referring to the snowball attack. We continued to explain to the policeman what we had been doing to amuse ourselves on a cold and boring January night.

"I wasn't on about that. We have had a phone call from your bar manager saying that he has been assaulted," he told us with the cheeky grin removed from his face. I thought he was referring to me grabbing the bar manager's arm and shoving him out of the door. With that, the bar manager appeared from inside.

"I want all the doormen from around the other bars and the hotel arrested for assault, affray and damage of property!" he started screaming. My partner and I stood there, flabbergasted at what this numpty was saying, and the copper looked at us and rolled his eyes. He looked at the manager and said,

"Sir, can you show me your bruises from the assault? Can you show me the damage of property? Because if you are referring to a snowball fight between doormen in this area, I think I'm going to arrest you for wasting police time!"

The bar manager stormed back into the bar, looking like he was about to cry. The policeman shook his head, touched the front of his helmet and gave it a little tilt forward and bade us a safe night as he turned and started to walk back to the van. I found the policeman very funny - his whole manner was a piss-take on the events as if he couldn't be arsed. He was obviously acting out his best Dixon of Dock Green impression. (GOOGLE HIM).

Next morning, the owner of the bar rang me and told me he had spoken to the bar manager and was going to have to let me and my partner doorman go because of our unprofessional manner of working the door the night before, I said to him, "Look, your manager was a little frosty last night. He needs to chill out. Have a think about it and ring me back midweek."

On Wednesday morning, I got a phone call from the owner of the bar telling us to go back to work as normal, so on the Friday night, we turned up to work to find the bar manager had suddenly resigned. He must have had a visit from the Abominable Snowman during the week!

Never boring even when it's boring.

24.

Bodge It and Scarper

One night on the door, it was late November 1998 and I was working this very busy nightclub. The owner at the time owned a few bars around our way and a few in other parts of the county. He owned garages and warehouses and he was involved in everything and anything that was going on; he was like a rich Del Boy. He had given me my first head doorman job at one of his bars in the area and he sorted me out with other bits and bobs to earn a bit of cash. At this particular time, I had been laid off from my daytime job as a rigger, as usual, just before Christmas time. It was always the same in that game; as long as the office staff got their Christmas bonus, sod the men on the tools.

So, this night I'd finished my work on my bar and then, to make my money up, I was going to work in the nightclub before going home. I was telling the lads I was working with about me being laid off, and as I was telling them, the owner of the club walked up and started having a yarn with us, found out I had been laid off from work and offered me a job in the refurbishment of the nightclub that was due to start the following week. I told him I was up for that. I was okay doing some labouring for builders, and when I was a lad, I used to play truant from school and work with my uncle from the age of 14 in the building game. Then, when I first left school, I was an apprentice bricklayer for 18 months. He was doing all his renovation work using the doormen who worked for him, so he got a good price and everybody was happy.

The following Monday morning, I went to start work on the nightclub and on the way, (well it wasn't on my way, it was out of my way but I like to be nice) I arranged to pick up one of the fellow doormen who was working with me. Now this guy was about 5ft 8" and about 8ft across and weighed a lot; I wouldn't like to guess and if he's reading this, I'd guess less! He came out of his house and got into my car; at that time, I was driving a red Vauxhall Calibra 2 litre 16v coupé sports car. He got in the passenger side... eventually, after huffing and puffing and shuffling, (if a blind man had been sat in the car he'd have thought a porno was going on) he got in and I realised I couldn't see out of the passenger side window! His belly had blocked any view I had. Not only that, my car had tilted considerably to one side. I was thinking, 'If the Old Bill stop me, I'm well in trouble for overloading my car.' We eventually arrived at the night club and started grafting. The job was going okay; don't think my car was enjoying the experience but it was a good laugh and the cash was going to help me out for Christmas. On the Wednesday morning, the owner turned up and said we needed the plasterers to work through the night on the men's toilet. The lads doing the plastering, Geoff and Paul, agreed to it no problem, and Paul asked me if I wanted to come in that night and help them out with labouring; Paul had known me from being a young boy working with my uncle on building projects.

"Yeah, sure, no probs," I told them. All the cash you can get for Christmas is appreciated, especially when you've got two daughters and a materialistic greedy wife.

"Right, we'll see you back here at 9, when the club opens," Paul told me,

"When the club opens?" I answered back, looking at Paul, wondering if I'd had heard him right.

"Yeah, Steve ain't shutting the club; he'll lose too much money. He's staying open," Paul grunted back to me through his half-open mouth. The other half of his mouth was gripping down on a fat cigar. I just walked off laughing, shaking my head, thinking, 'I don't fucking believe this'.

That night, I turned up at 9 pm on the dot to start work. The barmaids were there, the cashier/cloakroom attendant and, last but not least, a small door crew, as in numbers not in stature. During the week, it was a busy club, but not busy enough to justify a full crew of doormen to be working. I saw Paul and Geoff. "Right, what's the crack?" I ask them. Geoff replied, "Get yaself a JD; make it a double." He was on about a Jack Daniels. I got myself a JD the same as them and stood at the bar drinking it with them talking to the barmaids as the club started to fill up, but all the time I was wanting to crack on with the graft. Another double JD was slipped into my hand and then another. I was beginning to get a taste for staying out now; fuck the work. We got to about 10.30 and then Paul said, "Right, let's start boarding the walls and ceilings." I asked where the boards were, thinking they were going to be near the toilet area or actually in the toilets. No. Were they fuck! They were outside the back door near one of the bars! There were three bars in this nightclub, and the plasterboards were right across the other side of the club, a club that was now very busy. So, this is what happened next – unbelievable! Paul, Geoff and myself were now walking through the nightclub, half cut, with plasterboards on our shoulders. After the first run, the two of them decided to stay in the toilet and start nailing the boards to the ceiling, so they asked me to go back through the club and get some more plasterboards. Now, this is one of those experiences. When you think I've been all through loads of different adventures, sticky situations and scenarios on the door and never got flustered, but this one I was nervous about, walking through a nightclub in full swing now, half-cut on Jack Daniels, with plasterboards on my shoulder, just another crazy night in my life, I thought to myself as I set off walking to the other side of the nightclub in my ripped work-stained jeans, scruffy grey jumper, and mucky steel toe-capped work boots. I was walking through the revellers, trying not to bang into them with my plasterboard, getting loads of comments and funny looks. I mean, imagine being out in your best gear then in the morning you wake up and you have plasterboard dust on your clothes; imagine waking up and your partner is having a go at you for having plasterboard dust on your clothes, and you're telling them some story about a drunk workman who kept walking through the nightclub with plasterboards - it must have come from him! No partner is going to believe that and neither is any divorce judge, but that's what happened to a certain regular up the nightclub. Sorry about that.

So, eventually, I got through the crowd and back to the toilets where my two friends were waiting for me, drinking Jack Daniels and coke. They hand me a drink, telling me that one of the punters in the club had just bought them for us, and this went on all night - people were coming up and talking to us, offering us drinks. I'd finished bringing the plasterboards through the club and now started to mix the plaster to skim the ceilings. The only thing was I was fucking wrecked! I couldn't stand straight. I was that pissed I thought the doormen who were working were going to have to chuck me out for being pissed.

The time had come to shut the club and let the punters leave. After they had all gone, we decided to take a break from the graft and have a drink with the staff. This is something that happened in every venue I worked; after cashing up, all the staff had a drink together, unless the landlord was a tight bastard and you were never allowed a drink, which would happen at a few places I worked. So now, I was sat with the staff, topping up on JD and coke even more. The staff left and we locked the door behind them.

"Tell ya what," shouted Geoff, "let's have another drink before we start work again!" Paul agreed with Geoff that this was a good idea. I felt like crying but put on a macho image (a very pissed macho image) and agreed.

"Right, I'll pour the drinks, you put some music on, Matty," shouted Geoff as he went behind the bar reaching for the optics. Now, I'd never worked a set of DJ decks in my life at that time. I have since, but not then, and I wasn't sober. Once I had figured out how to turn it on, it looked like something out of Star Trek to me, flashing lights and knobs all over the place, I worked out how to put the CD in and then the sound and we were away; a bit of George Benson playing 'Gimme the Night'. I turned round to see Paul doing some dancing; he liked his Northern Soul, so he was doing that sort of moves; then I saw Geoff dancing. Now, here's the thing, Geoff was well known locally as a hard man, a bully, a miserable bastard etc., etc., I mean this guy had got me arrested some years before for fighting in a nightclub. He was not a dancer! He was doing moves like your drunk Granddad at a wedding, I was thinking I didn't believe it is happening.

"WOOOO! Matty, bang on some more tunes!" shouted Paul.

"Yeah, and I'll get some more drinks on!" shouted Geoff. More drinks? I'd never got to the last one! This scene kept repeating itself for the next hour or so until they were tired out, then Paul suggested we better go finish off the plastering in the toilet.

KNOCK, KNOCK, KNOCK! This came from the outside doors as some morning sunlight shone through the windows of the club. We'd only fallen asleep on the couches around the club! The toilets never got finished that night. The only thing that did get finished was the Jack Daniels! We had some explaining to do to the manager of the club when he came through the door and, later on that night, when we started the night shift again, to the owner of the club. The next few nights, we worked through the night in the toilets at the club, but this time there was no drinking. We still played our own music when the club was shut but the drinking was a big no. Besides, sometimes the bar staff would need a lift home at the end of their shift. Know what I mean?

25.

Lady in Red Is Chancing It with Me

One night on the door, I was working this nice little pub in the local suburbs. A few people had owned this pub over the years and tried to make a go of it, but it never seemed to do well for whatever reason; bit of a white elephant. Some guy from out of town bought it and tried different styles with it. The bar was split into two sides, one side of the pub before was twice, maybe three times the size of the other, and everybody who had owned the pub before the new owner had always made the larger side of the building the main bar for drinking, with the smaller catering for food. The new owner approached it differently and made the larger part for food. He served only quality fresh food and soon the restaurant part was taking bookings weeks then months in advance and the bar was becoming very popular within the local community, even though it had other very well-established pubs to compete with, one of them being literally across the road. The owner of the pub was a likeable sort of chap as well. So, as the pub began to grow in name and reputation, then obviously, the pub had to grow in size to compensate for trade and to make the owner more money.

While the work of the extension was being done, he got hold of me through a mutual friend to ask if I would run his door for him. To be honest, I was ready to give up working the doors at that time; I'd had enough. I was working in a nice place and was ready to retire from it all. I told him this during our phone call and he told me to give him the price I wanted for running the door for him, so I thought, 'I'm not really bothered', so I put quite a considerable mark-up on my normal rate. Straight away, he agreed! Best of it was, I later found out through our mutual friend that when he made that phone call to me, he was sat in my friend's car and after our phone conversation, he said he was willing to pay more. (DAMN!)

So, the new extension was completed and I started to run the door. It was a good little number, not really like other places I had run because the bar was full of locals and then, on a Friday and Saturday, there were doormen on, so If you had a problem with one of the locals and barred them, when you weren't there working during the week, they would go in the pub for a pint! Weird set up, but such is life. The bar became very popular and the owner started to put live acts on every Saturday night. I brought in another doorman to work with the one I was already working with. So now there were three of us working the door at the pub. Now, there was a problem festering with the local houses about the noise being made by the monster that had been created in this local suburb. There were noise complaints all the time, especially from this one woman. I got told she was a local councillor; I don't know about that, but what I do know is she was at it. I think she saw the pub doing well and jumped on the old blackmail train. See, I'd seen the bitch very briefly and like I said earlier, this pub had been there a long time, as had the pub across the road, probably before she was born, (JUST), so why, all of a sudden, complaints now?

We had the noise police round; we had to fix a monitor in the pub for the live acts on a Saturday night to make sure they never went over a certain noise level. We had all entertainment stopped at 11 pm on the dot and we had signs put up to ask all customers when leaving to please keep noise levels down and respect the people living in the nearby houses even though the ones closest to the pub never complained really, yet that silly bitch lived about 400 metres away, across a field behind some hedges and trees, and still complained! Fuck me, I thought we were going to end up giving out slippers to customers as they left the pub, or fitting silencers to exhausts as part of a meal deal! No matter what we did, the bitch moaned and moaned.

Obviously, like any job, you have to have a break and working the door is no different, especially with it being mainly Friday and Saturday nights. You get invites to parties, weddings, etc., etc., so one Saturday, I'd had a night off to attend some party, no probs. If anything ever happened when I wasn't working, I always found out the next day somehow, either from the gaffer of the pub, my door staff or some punter would tell me.

The following weekend I was back on the door, having a general chit chat with the boys, asking them if there had been anything exciting happening the week before. I knew there hadn't been any trouble or anything so I was just expecting a bit of chit chat back, then one of the lads starts telling me about our friendly councillor turning up and making a complaint about the noise; AGAIN!

"For fuck sake, don't that bitch have anything better to do with her life than fucking moan?" I said to one of the lads, shaking my head. They continued to tell me that they wouldn't let her into the premises and that she was causing a scene in the car park then being a nuisance around the patio area where people were drinking. They told her she would have to leave the grounds of the pub or they would have to ring the police. (If she had been a bloke, they wouldn't have bothered ringing the police, if you know what I mean). She carried on being a nuisance and then went to try and enter the premises round the back through the kitchen area. The doorman stopped her and she eventually gave up.

That night was a busy night. We had a Tom Jones tribute act on. He had performed at the pub a few times and he was a cheesy fucker of the highest standard, an old boy who had probably been on the circuit for years. I liked him; e entertained a crowd, got them involved and it was always a good night when he was on. So, he was on stage, giving it some and the audience were singing and we had one doorman outside and one inside watching the pub and I was floating about; easy number because you make it easy. I was stood talking to the doorman inside the pub, and Tom had just finished a song and leant down off the stage to one of the audience. Nothing out the norm with that; he's probably going to give her a kiss or accept a request for their favourite song, but just by looking at his face and then the reactions of the people stood around him, you could sense that something wasn't right, and I don't mean in the sense that the request was for him to strip off singing 'AGADOO' while juggling lemons!

Then my doorman partner nudged me and said,

"Fuck me, that's the councillor bird!" Now, all we can see is her head and shoulders (free dandruff shampoo welcome).

"Right, let's fucking have her out," I grunted as we started making our way through the crowd. I was well pissed off that she had got in past the lad on the door outside and past me and the other doorman stood just inside. As we got to where she was, I couldn't believe what I was seeing. She was only wearing a red dressing gown and pink fluffy slippers! She was in a pub making a complaint and she was wearing a red dressing gown and fluffy fucking slippers! Now, that was definitely a first and, to be honest, a last; I've never had it happen to me since.

"Look, love, you've got to leave," I said to her softly, placing my arm around her body space in a way to coax her out of the bar.

"I'm not going nowhere till he stops singing!" she squawked out, all emotional. Now the audience started booing her. Tom was being his usual professional self and just carried on talking to the audience. Our councillor started waffling on about noise levels and that she couldn't sleep, and I was trying to explain to her that we needed to discuss it outside. Then somebody did it; they only did it; it started and I knew it was going to come;

"Get ya tits out for the lads!!!" came one voice. By the second chorus, there were probably about 5 or 6, and by the third chorus, it was just about the whole pub. The councillor had lost it! She started to cry as she was ushered to the door. As we were walking through the crowded pub, young lads and men were asking her to get her tits out, leaning forward to ogle her. They genuinely thought she was a stripper! I was thinking to myself, 'I hope she's wearing something under this dressing gown because if a boob drops out, I'm not wearing my steel toe cap shoes tonight!' She looked a right frump to me, (mind you, been with worse; married worse, to be honest).

We got outside and I told her that this had got to stop now. She was blubbing away and, through her tears, it finally comes out what she was after.

"I want compensating; I can't sleep at night. This pub wasn't here when I moved into my house, so I'm going to keep doing this until I get some sort of compensation."

Why didn't she go and see the owner during the week or go through other channels? She was on the local council! It was because she wanted the old brown envelope as a sweetener; typical of somebody on a council. You can't keep having this kind of behaviour when you are trying to run a door, we all want an easy life, so I started doing some investigating and found out she had a couple of horses grazing in a field nearby. From what I heard, one morning when she visited her two horses, there were slippers on the horses which were wrapped in dressing gowns and a note saying;

'Your horses are keeping me awake with their noise. It is turning me to drink more at (name of pub), so if this continues, then TESCO will be receiving some more lasagne ingredients on the cheap!'

She never bothered us again and TESCO stopped selling lasagne of the horse variety.

EVERY LITTLE HELPS

26.

Gaffer Gets Spiked

One night on the door, I was working this club; it was a great place to work, always buzzing with great music, fights and dodgy dealings. It was just an endless rush of action-filled nights, and if you were somebody, you wanted to be there; there was all sorts of mischief going on. The owners of the club were a couple who, to be honest, just stayed together because it was cheaper than getting divorced. I mean, she was at it with doormen and anybody who was up for it, and he was the same, apart from the bit about the doormen, of course. So, on a normal night, she would stay downstairs on the cash desk and he would be upstairs in the club trying to dip his wick into anything he could. Most times, I would keep a lookout for him. I liked him and thought, 'Good luck to him'! Only thing was, the pair of them had no idea what the other was up to. By this, I mean that while he was upstairs, when the club shut its doors for the last hour of the night, all they had to do was double-lock a door which takes all of 5 minutes, and she wouldn't appear upstairs for about half an hour, if you know what I mean. What's good for the goose and all that carry on. The odd time, the pair of them would get suspicious of the other and there would be almighty arguments and fights between them, especially at closing time, which was great entertainment for the staff.

Sometimes, the woman of the relationship could be a right mardy bitch - probably wasn't getting enough, but the man -

he was always an optimist, always laughing. With the door work comes its perks, as you all will know, all jobs have their perks. Only thing was, if we were getting our perks while at work and the woman found out, she would get mardy and start to threaten us door staff with the sack. One night on the door, I got caught by the woman on the stairs getting some perks. She went absolutely ballistic, telling the head doorman that she wanted me sacked. He was doing his best to defend me; I don't know what he was saying or what he said but he should have been a solicitor because he managed to calm her down for a short while. At the end of the night, when the club was shut, she kicked off again! To be honest, it was her party piece - anything for a bit of attention. Her husband started agreeing with her! I couldn't fucking believe it - all the times I looked out for him, the fucking turncoat! I was raging more with him than her. All the times I had his back when he was up to no good! My mind was made up; he was going to feel some kind of retribution for his lack of loyalty.

The next night, we arrived at work, and the atmosphere between the door staff and the management was frosty, to say the least. I made my way upstairs and the owner came up and asked how I was. I told him I was fine, but inside, I still had the hump with him for his lack of loyalty. He cleared off towards the dance floor, as usual, chatting up the girls and getting them free drinks. When he would get the girls free drinks, he would sometimes afterwards progress onto the dance floor with them and have a boogie, and when he did this, he would ALWAYS leave his drink beside me, so I could keep an eye on it so nobody would spike him. If I had to leave my station to go and deal with something, I would tell him and his drink would get poured away.

Up came my gaffer, big smile on his face, and he asked me to look after his drink while he went for a dance. While he was dancing, I got on the radio to one of the other doormen who knew a bit about pharmacy at that time. I asked him to come upstairs because I might need assistance, One minute later, the doorman was stood beside me. I just nodded my head in the direction of the half-pint glass, he reached into his pocket and pulled out a clenched fist, glided his fist over the half-pint glass and then opened his hand. Plop! Something dropped into the glass and immediately sank to the bottom, causing the glass to make more bubbles, fizzing away. I was looking at the glass thinking, 'If the gaffer comes back now, he's going to suss this'. The gaffer returned to me about ten minutes later with a bit of a sweat on from dancing. He always wore a suit and tie, and this club would usually get humid with the body heat when it was busy.

"I'm having a great night," he said to me, smiling. He lifted up his glass and drank the remaining lager in three gulps. He let out a big sigh of contentment as he wiped his lips with the back of his hand.

"I'm off to get another drink and then I'm off for another dance. I reckon I've pulled. Let me know if the missus starts hovering about, won't ya?"

"Yeah, of course I will, no worries," I replied, thinking to myself, 'The only thing that is going to be hovering about is you in about half an hour, you fucking traitorous bastard.'

Fifteen minutes later, he was back, sweating like a judge round the back of King's Cross. He had chewing gum in his mouth which he was chewing away on like his life depended on it. He was all smiley and he was asking for his drink. I told him he drank it earlier. "Aww, fuck it, I'll drink this," he sprayed to me, as he picked up a half-pint of lager and continued to swallow it in one gulp, a big no-no back in those days; you never touched a drink unattended - you never know, it could be spiked! Off he went into the crowd of people, half walking, half dancing, the back of his suit soaking in sweat, like looking at the back of Alexander O'Neal in a suit, and that man sweats. Roughly ten minutes later, he was back again, this time he was gurning and sweating and asking me for his drink. I told him he hadn't got a drink, it was gone. He told me he loved me and that he was going to get a drink from the bar; basically, he was off his nut.

Over my radio came the voice of one of the doormen from downstairs; "We're cashing up down here now; we'll be upstairs in a mo." Now I know the shit is going to hit the fan once they come upstairs and the woman of the couple sees the state of her old man, then right in front of me there was a surge of people and the screams of women; it wasn't normal. I started thinking someone had either done a protein fart or let off CS gas! I ran towards the crowd, at the same time shouting down my radio to the doorman downstairs to come upstairs to assist me. As I pushed my way through the crowd in the direction of the incident, there was no stinging in my eyes which meant no CS gas and no stinging in my nostrils which meant no protein farts. To be honest, I think a protein fart is worse!

As I got through the crowd of screaming and giggling women and laughing men, I saw the gaffer of the club, naked on the dance floor, swinging his shirt around over his head! I stood there in shock not knowing how to cope with this. The other doormen arrived by my side seconds later and just cracked up laughing. The DJ was encouraging it all by getting the crowd to start clapping, then his missus turned up and she just launched herself at him with a barrage of punches! Now, we had to put a stop to this; it was getting to be a joke. We started to pull the pair apart and drag them to the office area. She was screaming her head off, trying to kick out at him. He was just laughing uncontrollably at her; the more she screamed and kicked, the more he laughed; the more he laughed, the more the door staff laughed. We got them both into the office and she started to throw office equipment about, pushing the computer off the desk. I just walked out of the office and left everybody to it. As I walked back through the club to my station, the place was bouncing. Everybody was smiling and laughing at what they had just been a witness to. I'd only been back at my station a matter of moments when the owner walked up to me with one of the other doormen. "What the fuck has gone on up here?" she asked me. "Why is he in such a fucking state? He's been fucking spiked!" she started screaming at me, waving her hands in the air.

"Look, it's his own fucking fault!" I shouted back at her, furious with the bitch who was now speaking to me like I was some kind of fucking idiot. "He picked up somebody else's drink earlier on and started to drink it. It must have been spiked!"

She stood there, paused and then looked to me and apologised, then went on to call him a fucking idiot. She started apologising for wanting to sack us and called us good doormen for how we always looked after her and her husband. She said how she was thinking of giving us all a pay rise, then she gave me a kiss on the cheek and walked off. I leant towards the doorman who had been stood beside her and whispered in his ear, "Fuck me, what's got into her? She's never that nice!" As I leant back to wait for his response, he just gave me a wink and said,

"You know the saying, Matty, what is good for the goose is good for the gander, if you know what I mean."

"Fuck!"

27.

Do It Yourself

One night on the door, I was working this club which was always quiet until the local pubs and bars used to shut, then it would be packed out. We used to start work with all the crew stood on the front door, then half of us would go upstairs and leave half the crew downstairs on the door. This one Friday night, I'd gone upstairs with half the crew and as we got into the main foyer of the club, we saw a man and a woman arguing; nothing out of the ordinary, but still needed to be nipped in the bud. One of the lads went over and had a word with the couple to calm things down, and they did, which, trust me, is a rarity in the pub game. As they walked off, the woman gave a flirtatious smile in our direction, so we all smiled back. I asked the doormen if they knew her. One of the lads informed me that she worked in one of the local DIY mega-stores, which, at that time, got my full attention. I was 22 and had bought my first house, a repossession that needed a full scope of renovation, so between my daytime job, door jobs, training, raising finances for a wedding and raising a young daughter, in what spare time I had left, I was making a house a home. I had an uncle who was a builder so we would do favours for favours and he would do work on my house for me, but obviously I had to buy the materials, or shall we say acquire the materials.

Like every job in the world, you've got to have your perks. If a job hasn't got any perks, then you should be jacking it in. I was a hunter and I had my sights on my prey. Later on in the night, the woman walked past. I ask her how she was doing and she told me she was doing okay; that would do for now; the seed had been sown.

You see, I don't know how to chat a girl up, still don't, but I knew I needed some kind of connection with this girl to see if we could do favours for favours, ya know, I let her and her boyfriend in the pubs and clubs for nothing, let them enter straight away so they don't have to queue and maybe she can get me a bit of a discount at her workplace; maybe a lot of discount; fuck it, let's be honest, I was wanting 100% discount! So, throughout the night, I was strategically placing myself in different locations in the club, so I always seemed to be in her line of sight, catching a glimpse of her, the odd smile. Some of you reading this are probably thinking I was flirting, but I can assure you I wasn't; it was strictly business on my behalf. A few times throughout the night, her boyfriend caught her looking in my direction, so then he started positioning himself strategically so our view of each other was blocked. You know what? Come to think of it, I can't believe there isn't a dance routine called the 'STRATEGICALLY POSITIONING' because, let's be honest, it goes on all the time in pubs and clubs between men and women. I could see in her boyfriend's face he was starting to get the hump with all this shifting, shuffling and 'STRATEGICALLY POSITIONING'. They both left the club with a group of people well before closing time, and that was it; I thought my chance of some discounted DIY gear was blown.

The night in the club was going well; no trouble, which was good for this club. Ss the DJ started to play the 'erection section' of music. In those days, in certain clubs, we referred to the slow dancing at the end of the night between a boy and a girl hugging each other really close (or probably leaning on each other to stay standing because they were pissed) as the 'erection section', which was quite a contrast to working a rave club in those days, as they always used to finish on a huge up-tempo beat. As the music was playing, one of the doormen came up to me and told me there was some girl at the front door asking for me. I asked him to cover for me while I went to check it out. I got to the front door and saw the girl who worked in the DIY store!

"I don't want to sound cheeky, but can you do me a favour?" she asked me with a smile.

"Yeah, sure, no problem," I replied, running a shopping list through my head.

"Well, me and my boyfriend have had an argument and he's left me and I have no money to get home in a taxi…" Before she could finish her sentence, I was taking no chances on her asking for money for a taxi; I was straight in quicker than a nail gun. "I'll give you a lift".

I nipped off to find the head doorman to let him know I was sneaking off, and he was sound about it.

Myself and the girl walked away from the club to where my car was parked.

"What do you do for a living, then?" I asked her.

"I work in the new mega DIY store on the new retail park."

"Oh, really?" I replied with my best look of surprise. "Do you enjoy your job?"

"It will do for now."

I started the car and asked her where we were going, did she live with her boyfriend, when was she next back at work?

With the number of questions I was asking her, the poor girl must have thought she had got in a car with the police! She told me where we were going, explained that she didn't live with her boyfriend, and that she was at work in the morning.

"Oh, really? I might pop into your workplace in the morning; I'm renovating a house," I told her, hoping she was going to offer me some discount, or at least offer me something; I mean it was 2 in the morning and we were adults in a car and I was a doorman, and even though she didn't work at 'SCREWFIX', for some reason that DIY store kept running through my mind.

"Yeah call in in the morning and I will sort you out," she said as we pulled up near her house. I parked my car, then there was that awkward moment of silence when we were both probably wondering what to do. She leant over and gave me a kiss on the cheek, and whispered, "Thanks for the lift but I got to go now. I got to be up early for work. Don't forget to come and see me at work and I will sort you out".

Now, the next morning, I was up early. My uncle picked me up in his transit van. We did our usual Saturday morning routine; got down the builders' merchants, got down the timber yard as soon as they both opened, when most, if not all the staff were nursing their heads from a Friday night on the booze. It was at this glorious time that myself and my uncle would make our own kind of discount on materials. I told my uncle about the night before with the girl who worked in the new DIY megastore, who said she would sort me out, and he told me that was mad because a guy who went to his snooker club had just started there as a security guard! As he finished explaining this to me, we both looked at each other and thought the same.

We went into the DIY megastore and there, by the door, was standing a podgy, wispy-haired security guard, whose body manner was saying, 'I've got no confidence'. He was a shirt-filler for some security company. Now, I don't know about putting a shoplifter out, but this security guard didn't look like he could put a cigarette out. We said hello to the security guard and proceeded into the store where we split up. I walked up and down a couple of the aisles and grabbed some bits and bobs for my renovation project, and then spotted the girl from the night before, or should I say, a few hours before.

"Now then, you look fresh on not many hours sleep," I told her, which she did to be honest.

"Thanks. You look like you're going to be busy today," she said, looking at my bits and bobs. "Come over here and I will sort you out," she said, walking off.

Now, all the time she had been saying 'I will sort you out', I was taking this to mean a discount, so I didn't grab too many bits and bobs until I knew what kind of discount I was getting. She led me to the outdoor section where they keep fencing, plant pots, all that kind of Charlie Dimmock shit, and where they also keep sheds. She walked up to one of these sheds and opened the door. "Come and look inside this shed," she said to me with a smile that would melt concrete. I went in and we shut the door. All I will say from this point is, I don't know one shed from another but that was definitely a potting shed and as for a discount on my bits and bobs, I never paid a penny. She tucked them away for me before I came out of that potting shed. I eventually got sorted out, I thanked the girl for her customer service and discount and promised I would definitely return.

I got to my uncle's van outside and he was sitting there waiting for me, pissed off.

"Where the fuck have you been? I've been waiting for fucking ages! Did she sort you out with a discount? And what the fuck are you smiling for?" I told him what had just happened in the DIY store.

That night on the door, the girl showed up with her friends, I told them to come straight to the front of the queue, and when I let them in, I told the cashier that my friend didn't have to pay, as she was on my guest list, and that's the way it went on for months. I left strict instructions on the door that my new-found friend NEVER had to pay to enter, even if I wasn't working on a night she showed up, I would sometimes get the bar staff to give her free drinks, and I went shopping early every Saturday morning and turned a repossessed house into a palace with all the bits and bobs I had sorted out.

I never bothered getting a potting shed, though, I ended up building one! I actually wrote a poem about the shed I built; I wonder if I should write a poem about the shed at the DIY megastore?

28.

Drunkrobics

One night on the door, I was working this venue, a nice little regular earner on a Thursday night. At the beginning of the night, there would be 5 to 6 of us working the venue. It used to be, in the early days of cheap drink promotions, this venue would do cheap drinks up to 11 o'clock, even though it was open until 1 am, then the clientele would start to move on to one of the local clubs in the area that would also be doing a promotion. It was a good place to work, good DJs doing sets and rarely any trouble considering it was a young crowd. As the crowd would filter down, the head doorman would let a few of us leave early. I say early, but the head doorman was tighter than a duck's arse; let's just say if you left at 10.59 pm you got paid till 10.59 pm. If your wages came to twenty-four pounds and ninety-nine pence, you'd be reading this thinking I am going to be getting twenty-five pounds in my wage packet. No chance! I got twenty-four pounds and ninety-nine pence. I don't know if he still charged the gaffer of the venue for full shifts for the night even though he paid us to the minute; none of my business, to be honest. If he was, good luck to him.

Every time he let doormen go early, he would always ask me to stay. Sometimes there would be just me and him working the venue, and sometimes we would get caught out by a late-night surge of people coming into the venue, but we were lucky as we never had any major incidents to deal with. You see, at that time of night, more people are pissed - would like to put iniberated but I can't spell it - and as we all know, when people are pissed, there is more chance of trouble, but we did ok. Plus, the head doorman was very strict on letting people re-enter at that time of night if they seemed a little worse for wear, and I do mean a LITTLE worse for wear. Fuck me, if you were wearing a pair of shoes and one shoe had a heel 2mm higher than the other heel, causing you to walk funny, you weren't getting in. If you had a limp, you weren't getting in; fuck it, if you had a wonky fringe this head doorman was not letting you in, he was that strict. He wasn't doing it in a malicious way or like some doormen I had worked with, doing it for a power trip, he just felt the need towards the end of the night to be very strict about letting people enter, especially the youngsters.

Now, all this being strict was a bit new to me. I'd worked places before here, and still was at the time, where the only rules they enforced was that you were wearing clothes and you paid for your drink. Sometimes, they didn't apply in the places that were rough. So, if, on the rare occasion, I would be stood on the door on my own and some young student turned up at the door, I would let them in. The way I looked at it, it was towards the end of the night. Of course, they were going to be pissed and if they didn't look like aggro, no harm done.

Now if the head doorman was stood with me, he'd be saying "Not tonight, mate, you've had enough." Sometimes I thought he was right, other times I thought he was probably a bit harsh, but I had to stand by his decisions - it was his club. Hey, don't get me wrong; I wouldn't work anywhere if I totally disagreed with the rules and thought they were out of order but it this wasn't a big deal, to be honest. That also applied to my daytime work as well, as anybody who has worked with me will tell you.

So here is what I used to do to try and diffuse any difficult situations that might become confrontational, and, more often than not, it went like this.

The head doorman would stop the lad/bloke/man - funny that, he always stopped the males, never ever any females - they would start to moan and complain, things would start to become heated, I would then act as a peacemaker and say, "Well, he doesn't look too bad, to be fair," but because I didn't want to go against the head doorman's authority and look like I was siding with the punter, who by now already liked me because he thought I had taken his side, I would then ask the punter to start doing an array of tasks to prove they could be let in, which they would always do for me because I was on their side. I usually started with the 'close your eyes and put your left-hand or right-hand index finger to your nose' routine. I only used to do that because I'd seen it on the TV programme 'COPS' on the CBSS channel. Then, I'd probably get them to stand on one leg. Now remember, I was not doing this to belittle anybody, it's not in my nature. I was doing this to defuse a situation, having a laugh with the punter and at the same time making the head doorman become relaxed and not so harsh because they'd had a few. I can't remember a single time when this kind of game-playing went wrong and the punter never ended up getting into the venue for a few more drinks; everybody had a laugh.

Such is life, and like anything in life, lifting a hand to a nose or standing on one leg became boring, so each week another task would be introduced or added to the routine. Honest to

God, we had them doing press-ups, star jumps, burpees, and all sorts of other exercises. I was getting ideas from my boxing training. If there was more than one of them, we would have them race up and down the street. First one back got a free drink or free entry. We'd have them doing wheelbarrow races; now remember, these were lads on a night out in some of their best clobber. One night, there was just me and the head doorman stood there and three lads walked up and just started doing star jumps. Everybody just cracked up laughing and we let them enter the venue for free. Some working contractors from the North East were about to enter the venue as this happened. They started laughing along at what they had just seen. Now, you might read this and be thinking 'you'd never get me doing that shit to enter a club'. Hey, I totally agree with you, I fucking wouldn't do that shit either. I wasn't belittling people; it was just something that started out as harmless fun and became a little bit legendary as a funny thing to do to get into that venue after a certain time, especially amongst the younger lads. Fuck me, sometimes on a Thursday night before I left my house, I used to think to myself, 'Shall I wear a monkey suit or shall I wear lycra?' I could have started a new craze - drunkrobics!

29.

Paras Letic

One night on the door, I was working this venue. It was a venue I have referred to many times before in this book, and like I have said before, I won't be naming places or people to protect the innocent and the guilty, but for this story, by the time I have described the surrounding area and the events that happened that night, it won't be hard to figure out which venue I am talking about. It was a Thursday night and it was busy. The venue was in a line of other bars and clubs down a strip. As you walked down the strip, on one side you had nightclubs and bars and on the other side, you had a barrier measuring approximately 4ft high. On the other side of the barrier was about a 20ft drop into the water. This small area of water also had a barge anchored up there which was also a bar. Funnily enough, it was known as 'the barge'! I think I've only ever visited the barge once in my life, in my teens.

I had three of us working this Thursday night- never any less than three on a Thursday. Sometimes it would have warranted having four doormen with the amount of trouble we got in there. One of the doormen was also a friend from my daytime job. We had worked together on different projects around the area and also around the country. He was alright as a doorman; I've worked with better and worked with worse. The only problem was he lied all the time! Honestly, he was that good a liar he could be telling me and the other doormen a story and I would know he was lying, but by the end of the story, I fucking believed him. He made Walter Mitty look like Honest John! This doorman had no problem pulling women. I used to tell the blokes at work in my daytime job and they didn't believe me. I told them it stood to reason; he pulled women because he told them lies and they believed him. I'm not saying he was God's gift; I'm stating a fact that he pulled women, but once they sussed him out, they dumped him. Probably dumped him on a Monday when he's trying to tell them it's a Thursday and he's got to nip out to bell Prince Charles on the way to picking up his Millennium Falcon that he was having serviced with the Pope Mobile because he had got a deal on 2 4 1 vouchers given to him by the Prime Minister last time he was at Downing Street giving the PM some advice. The 2 4 1 voucher they probably wouldn't believe, but he would have had them believing the rest of the story. ...I did.

So, we were busy and it was a good atmosphere, no tension, everybody having a good time. The three of us would all stand together on the door and we could all scope the venue pretty well from the main door. We might have to stand on an empty beer crate (old school habit, none of that now with HSE, be classed as working at height) to get a better view around the place now and then, but no problem. The place was like a big airport lounge, and to be honest, if it wasn't for the great DJ they had working there, it would probably have never taken off (like that - see what I did there?).

We saw a lad take off his top and start dancing naked from the waist up. He was a fit lad, early 20s, and we all made a move to go over together.

"It's okay," I said to the other two, raising my arm to stop them. "I'll deal with it." I went over to the lad and asked him to put his T-shirt back on. The young man was very happy to do so and apologised; straight away I liked him - you could tell he wasn't trouble, just mischievous. Nothing wrong with that, but I was working and I had a job to do. Roughly ten minutes later, his top was off again. We went through virtually the same motions - all three of us moved from the door in his direction, I told the other doormen, "It's okay, I'll deal with it," and when I reach the young man, he apologises, laughing, but not laughing in a piss-take way, and puts his T-shirt back on. The young man was in high spirits. When I got back to the other doormen standing by the entrance, they explained that when I was having a word, they had realised there were six of them in this group. My friend who liked to tell the odd porky told me if he did it again he was having him out. I thought to myself, 'We'll have our work cut out with these six'. Just something about them was bothering me, not in a nasty way, but you just got that feeling sometimes about situations. Fuck me, he took it off a third time!

"Leave it, I'll have a word and tell him if he does it again, he's going to have to go," I was telling the other two as I set off to deal with my male stripper friend. As I approached, another two of his friends took their T-shirts off. Then I saw it, and I couldn't believe I hadn't picked up on it the two times before - they had the Parachute Regiment tattoo! Anybody who defends my country has my respect, but still, I have a job to do. I asked them all to put their T-shirts back on and like the two times before, they had a bit of banter with me and put their T-shirts back on. I explained that they would have to leave if they carried on removing their T-shirts, but it fell on deaf ears. It must be all those hand grenades. Once again, I returned to the door and the other two doormen were looking pissed off.

"You should have them out. They're taking the fucking piss," said one of the doormen, all screwed-up face, bulldog, thistle, chewing, get my gist? I didn't bother telling the other two doormen about the Para tattoos; couldn't be arsed with them the way they thought I wasn't dealing with the situation properly. Hey, they might have been right, but fuck 'em, I was head doorman, and I didn't want any trouble. Besides, the girls were loving their free strip show every ten minutes!

About ten minutes later, I saw a friend walk past outside the venue. I nipped out to engage in a friendly discussion with my friend and see what their intentions were later on. As I was talking to my friend outside the venue, out the corner of my eye, I saw a bundle of male flesh and monkey suit come stumbling out the door. Sure enough, it was my male stripper friend with his T-shirt off and one of the doormen. "He's out this time," said the doorman, gasping for breath. The young man wasn't even bothered, he was too busy laughing. With that, the other doorman appeared with another one of the crowd with his T-shirt off. Walking behind them was another two of the group walking behind them with their T-shirts off just laughing. There was no malice, no agitation, these paras proper didn't give a fuck; they just kept laughing. I approached the lead stripper and told him he would not be allowed in the venue any more. He just started laughing and, nice as pie, said to me, "No probs, mate. Thanks for a good night but I fancy a swim anyway," and with that, he took three steps towards the barrier, placed his hands on the top and did one of these jumps where you swing your legs to the side and over the top.

Splash!!! Fuck me, he's in the water! I ran to the barrier with a host of other people and the two doormen looked over the top and there he was, paddling away, and of course, laughing. To the left side of me, I saw two more bodies jump over the barrier. For a split second, I thought it was a pair of David Hasselhoff wannabes, but only for a split second because before the bodies hit the water, I knew it was our male stripper-turned-mermaid friends! Now there were three of them in there, paddling away on their backs, laughing and swimming. People started cheering and laughing. SPLASH!!! And now we have four of them swimming and splashing about. At one point, I thought they were going to break into synchronized swimming; now that would have been funny. Within a short space of time of this all going on, the police were on the scene, pushing people about looking for someone to blame, asking if the doormen had chucked them over the barrier, and at the same time, shouting at our synchronized swimmers to get out, to make to the ladder, to find a safe way to get out of the water, not to panic. There had been an incident earlier in the year before I worked down at the venue, where a man had fallen into the water and was lucky to survive apparently. It was in the local paper how a policeman had dived in to save him; the police were saying how dangerous it was, blah, blah, blah. Oh, really? When I was a kid, myself and most of my friends off the estate used to swim in there, as well as other kids from different parts of town.

So, the police went running around to the other side of the water where there was a slope, and by now, they have realised that these lads weren't going to get out of the water. They were, as usual, laughing; such a jolly bunch. While the police were shouting threats of arrest and how they could get eaten by sharks and crocodiles, the two other lads who were with their party came up and leant on the barrier beside me. They started shaking their heads.

"Them Old Bill won't get them out of the water, mate, they're not giving a fuck. We're off to Afghanistan soon, so do you think we or them give a fuck about anything? We're just living it up!" he told me, laughing. At the same time, the night air was full of laughter and cheers from the walkways from all the people walking by the water babies. The police were getting irate, helmets were off and threats were getting more serious, and all the time, guess what? They were still laughing.

"You take care out there in Afghanistan; come back safe," I said to the young man next to me as I reached out my hand to shake his hand.

"Thanks, mate, I will do," he replied as we shook hands. "By the way, tell your other doorman friend he's full of shit; he's never been in the SAS!"

"Oh, really? I fucking believed him," I whispered to myself as I walked back to the entrance of the venue wondering what the fuck had just happened, with the sound of laughter echoing in the night air.

30.

Clothes Sale

One night on the door, on a Friday night, I was working this venue; it was a bank holiday weekend. One of the punters came in - a nice bloke, local businessman, a bit dodgy (tell me a businessman who isn't), and asked how things were going. He asked me if I was working the door all weekend. You see, on a bank holiday weekend, a Sunday night was probably the busiest night, so I told him, "Yeah, I'm working all weekend." He asked me if I was interested in working the Sunday afternoon for him as he had hired a venue for a designer clothes sale. He continued to tell me that he didn't realise that the local football team had a friendly on, with a team that always brought a good turnout to the area, and which always produced a lot of trouble at the match and surrounding areas, including around the area of the venue he had hired, so naturally, now he had to worry about football hooligans steaming his sale as well as the local shoplifters. We agreed a price, a starting time and a finishing time and that I should get some other doormen to work with me doing the security.

On Sunday morning at 10 am, I turned up at the venue to start doing the door security. It was a hot Sunday morning and you could tell it was only going to get hotter. Thankfully, when I agreed to do the security for this event, he was happy for myself and the other lads not to be wearing our monkey outfits (what they used to call the old black suit and dickie bow attire that the doormen wore in those days). I had one doorman working with me from 10 am until 1 pm and then he would get off and another doorman came to work with me till they decided to shut the doors on the sale, no later than 5 pm. Nice one; everybody got a share, as it should be.

Now here's the thing; remember me saying about the football match and the trouble expected? Well, I knew that two lads on a door weren't going to stop a gang of hooligans steaming into them. The only thing you can do is shut the doors before they get to you, but what if they play it cool and send one or two at a time in and then just gang up and take what they want? We could try and stop them but I very much doubted we would get a result, maybe a good beating but we wouldn't be able to stop them. So, this time, I took a few precautions on the door. We had a few tools behind the door just in case things went a bit Pete Tong. The doorman who worked the first part of the shift with me brought in a tin of CS gas. I wasn't really keen on the CS gas because it was classed as a firearm and if you sprayed CS gas, the charge at that time came under a terrorist act (poisoning society). But it was there now so I told him to put it behind the door with the tools.

It was a nice sunny Sunday morning and the sale was going okay. I think the businessman was a bit disappointed with the turnout, but for me, as long as there were no signs of any football hooligans or shoplifters about, I was happy; I always liked to earn easy money. At 12.50, the other doorman turned up to start his part of the shift. He told us about his adventures at Sunday School that morning, then we all engaged in a conversation about the weekend's antics on the door and the usual bullshit that all doormen talk about - the ex-wife, shagging, fighting, protein diets and Coronation Street. One o'clock came and the first doorman got himself off ready to catch up on the EastEnders omnibus. The clothes sale started to get busy, a good crowd but nothing for us to worry about. I told the doorman working with me, "I'm just nipping off to the toilet for a number 2. I'll be as quick as I can and there are some tools behind the door just in case you need them".

I walked through the crowd of people towards the toilets and saw the businessman had a broad smile and was happy with the crowd at the venue. I walked through one set of doors and then another set of doors, and then I entered the cubicle and shut the door behind me. The cubicle door was one of the doors that spanned from top to bottom, the kind sniffers love. I dropped my trousers and took a seat, got out my phone, checked my Facebook, Twitter, E-mail and of course my stock market shares. Done, feeling half a stone lighter, I went through the routine of cleaning myself up, opened the cubicle door, went to the basin and washed my hands, checked my extremely good looks in the mirror, and headed for the door. I walked through the door and everything in the room where the sale was going on looked just how it had before I went to the khazi; people browsing and buying and no trouble.

I got back to the door and stood with my partner and went on to tell him about the CS gas I had with me. He started laughing and said, "Let me see it," so I handed the canister over to him and he grabbed it in his hand and started to rotate his hand, admiring it like a jeweller admiring a diamond. As he was fondling and caressing the CS gas canister, he somehow managed to push the button which let out a spray of gas, right into his face! Immediately, he screamed and dropped the canister. I was just about to start laughing at the stupid bastard, but before I could, the gas had managed to expand into the atmosphere and fucking expand right into my face! To be more precise, it had expanded right into my eyes, so now I started screaming! I knew not to rub my eyes because that would make it worse. My eyes were shut now and I couldn't see. I was in agony, and all I can hear is my partner moaning in agony too.

"You fucking tool, you fucking absolute fucking tool!" I shouted out towards my partner.

"Why, what have I fucking done?" he shouted back to me somewhere from my left side.

"What the fuck have you done? What the fuck have you done? Are you fucking kidding me?" Before he could reply, there was a new sound shrilled out, like a cross between a moan and a scream. I knew straight away it was some unsuspecting person who had walked into the CS gas cloud that was floating about. I say cloud; it was probably a few particles but to me and my stinging face, it was bigger than the cloud above Hiroshima. Then we heard another scream, and another, it was like a domino effect of screams and moans. I was trying to open my eyes but at the same time think how I was going to explain to the businessman we were working for what had happened to cause this carry-on. Somebody turned up with a jug of water and started to tip my head back and pour the water gently into my eyes. It didn't take away the stinging even though it did ease the pain a bit. My sight started to come back a little, even though it was a bit blurry. I managed to see the canister on the floor, reached down and picked it up. I leant my body just outside the doorway and chucked the canister into the guttering just above the doorway. As I turned round and looked round the foyer, people were bent over coughing and spluttering and moaning and screaming. I thought to myself, 'Fuck me, you never used to see this in the sales on 'Are You Being Served'! Never mind "I'm Freeeeee", more like "I can't seeee".

A few minutes later, the businessman who hired us turned up and asked me what had gone on. "People won't come to spend money if they see all this going on; it looks like a fucking war zone."

I nodded my head and agreed with him, and carried on to tell him how a very large group of football hooligans from away tried to storm the doorway to get in and rob his clothes sale which would have cost him thousands of pounds in lost goods and that if it hadn't been for the quick thinking of my partner, holding them back with his martial arts skills after being sprayed with CS gas, then what he was watching now was nothing to what could have been.

Inside, I was feeling quite happy with myself and smug at the brilliant excuse I had just come up with. All I needed to do now was get to my partner to get him all sorted out to tell the same story. I didn't get a chance to though; the businessman walked over to him. I could see my partner looking at him through his red eyes, a bit mystified. I couldn't hear what was being said but I saw the businessman put something into my partner's hand and pat his back and walk off.

I immediately walked over to my partner and asked what had just gone on. My partner looked at me and said,

"That bloke who's gig it is just thanked me for saving him a load of money, then give me 50 quid!" My partner looked at me in bewilderment and carried on to say, "Do you think it's because, with me letting the gas off, people couldn't leave so had to buy more clothes?"

"Yeah, could be, mate, could be," I sighed, shaking my head, walking off back towards the door thinking, 'This is UNFUCKINBELIEVABLE - the guy poisons everybody here, including himself, and then gets 50 quid extra for doing it'.

31.

Burger, Fries and Illegal Highs

One night on the door, I was working this venue, a proper rave place. At the time, it was expensive to get in, because hardly any money was made on the bar. Alcohol was hardly sold at a rave - it was only soft drinks and water, a lot of water, to the point where the boss of the venue would turn off the taps in the toilet. This place was full of drugs, mugs and thugs, dealers, squealers and feelers and full of gurners. I swear they gurned that much, 20 years later I see them around town and they're still gurning. There was never any trouble; easy money; everybody danced and loved each other.

So, this one night, a burger van pulled up across the road outside this venue to do business. We all started laughing and went over to explain to the burger van owner that they wouldn't get any business here. Nobody eats; their mouths might be moving all the time but they are empty. As we approached the burger van, two men get out of the front driver's cab. Immediately, I recognised one of them, a bit of a local character, into all sorts, very charismatic and straight away I sussed it out - it wasn't about selling burgers, hot dogs and all that carry on, this was going to be a front to launder money! For this story, I will call our very charismatic friend 'Ronald'.

"Alright, lads, how's it going?" said Ronald, smiling. He then cracked a joke. You couldn't help but like this guy. "Let me get heated up and I will do you some food and a cup of coffee."

He jumped into the back of the van, lifted his shutter, turned on his lights and started to get to work making food. I don't know why because he was never going to sell any food outside this venue. Myself and the other doorman walked back to the front door of the venue, discussing what 'Ronald' was up to, laughing amongst ourselves at his antics.

A few minutes later, Ronald shouts from the burger van.

"Alright, gents, what you wanting to eat? I've knocked you up some burgers and fries!"

"No, thanks," replied the head doorman. "Three coffees will do us!"

We had a good head doorman at this venue, always professional, he wasn't that keen on the lads chewing gum, probably because, if you were chewing gum, you blended in with the ravers and looked like a gurner. Ronald sent his mate over with the three coffees, while he just stood in the back of the van constantly talking on his mobile phone. A mobile phone was a rarity back then; politicians, the rich and dealers mainly had them. Ronald didn't wear a suit and patronise people, so he was definitely not a politician, he didn't show signs of being rich, so he had to be a dealer.

We started getting near closing time. A car drove up behind the burger van and parked up, then out got a dodgy character. I could tell he was dodgy by his walk, the way he was walking carrying invisible carpets under his arms and muscles bulging through his top that was two sizes too small for him; obviously a steroid head. He approached the burger van and said something I couldn't quite hear. He looked like he was ordering food. Ronald turned around, looked like he was cooking something, turned back around and passed to the steroid head what looked like a burger, which steroid head took with one hand and with the other hand passed over a wad of notes. Now, I don't know how much was in the wad, but that was some pricey burger! Steroid head walked back to his car, looked over to where we were on the door and gave a leery smile, a smile I'd seen a million times before and a million times after. It was the smile of a plastic gangster - earns a few quid doing drugs but struts around like he's the new 'Tony Montana'. He got in his car and drove off.

Less than five minutes later, another car turned up, parked behind the burger van, and another wannabe carpet-fitter got out of his car and walked up to the burger van. Then we see a repeat of buying an expensive burger and a big bundle of cash handed over, then the walk back to the car with the leery look to us doormen. Less than five minutes later, it happened again. We on the door didn't mind him doing what he was doing; we never had a say in it, to be honest. What he got up to on the streets was none of our business. It was up to the police to deal with him, and that was the point; if he had parked outside our venue doing his business, then eventually, the police would be on to him and start watching his goings-on and from there, start seeing whatever we on the door were up to, not that we were up to anything or doing anything wrong.

Ronald kept looking over to us stood on the door and smiling. He was constantly smiling. He had one of those cheeky 'I don't give a fuck' smiles, then he started to play some dance music from his burger van. Another car pulled up; Ronald was dancing about the van with not a care in the world. You could see the smoke billowing from the serving hatch and every now and then the smell of food. I had no idea why he was bothering to cook food; he was never going to sell any food outside a rave club; nobody eats. We were getting near to closing time so, as normal, we started to get taxis arriving. Sure enough, the first taxi arrived. The driver got out of his car and approached the burger van. He asked for a cup of tea and a burger; the look on the face of Ronald was class. You could see he didn't want to serve him. He was still smiling and carried on to serve the taxi driver. A few minutes later, the taxi driver received his burger, took a bite and gave it a nod of approval. As he carried on chomping his way through his burger, another two taxis pulled up. He shouted over to them to come and try the burgers before the venue started to empty out, so the two taxi drivers got out of their cars and approached the burger van hatch and placed an order. Our friend Ronald rolled his eyes while still smiling and began cooking their order. The last song of the night was playing in the venue; we had to leave the door now and deal with the customers inside and start to get ready to ask them to leave, which used to be a hard task alone, just because they always had a good night and just wanted to carry on dancing the night away. They were always in high spirits; well, they were definitely high in spirit as well as everything else. We start to get the ravers to exit the venue which, surprisingly, on this night was going quite easily, then I realised that word was getting passed back that there was a burger van outside playing music, so the ravers began to surround the burger van and start dancing. It was quite a sight to see! There were ravers dancing and taxi drivers eating, there were still the roid heads pulling up doing whatever they were up to with Ronald; it was like a scene out of a dance movie, everybody enjoying themselves apart from obviously the nearby residential houses. You could see lights begin to switch on, the movement of curtains, and it was pretty obvious to us doormen what was going to happen next. Sure enough, it did! A police car and a police riot van turned up, and as they did, the owner of the burger van must have thought they were coming to arrest him, because he opened the back door and ran off, followed by a roid head. As he left the burger van, he left the back door open. Two of the ravers from the club went through the back door and started to act as if they were serving. The police didn't notice the owner of the burger van running off, so as they approached the serving hatch, they just saw two sweaty, unhygienic men looking like they have had a busy night.

"Right, who's the owner of this burger van? Turn that music off now!! Have you got an entertainments licence for playing that music? Have you got any paperwork from the council for pitching here? I want to see it right now!" shouted the police officer in command. The two raving men just looked at the policeman and carried on swaying to the music with a little less gurning on their faces. The taxi drivers, who were stood to the side of the burger van, started to giggle to themselves, which made the police officer in charge get irate.

"Right, you had your chance to comply," he shouted, turned to his accompanying back-up of police officers, which had now grown since the arrival of another police car and riot van, and told them to turn off the music and shut down the burger van and continue to arrest the two men inside. Still, while all this was going on, the ravers were dancing, wanting to hug the police officers and show them some love.

We on the door couldn't believe that the police officer in charge had not got the savvy to see that the two men were obviously out of it and it would not be their burger van. The police arrested the two men, grabbed them and cuffed them and led them to the police van. The two men put up no resistance; they didn't speak, they just gurned, and still, we couldn't believe that none of the police had realised they couldn't cook a round of toast, never mind run a burger van. The police continued to turn off the music and shut down all the appliances on the burger van. While all this was going on, we were hanging around waiting for the police to make some kind of discovery, a major drugs haul, a big cash find, but nothing. The ravers were starting to disperse now the music had stopped. The police were talking amongst themselves about having to drive the burger van away or leave it there for the night locked up, because they had searched the two men before putting them in the back of the van and found no keys. They decided to look around the cab to try and find some keys, and of course, they ended up finding a wad of cash and some bags of illegal substances and a bag with some pills in. The police were so happy I thought they were going to start necking the pills and having their own party (has been known, read that story later). The other van and car got called away to a disturbance. The two officers remaining with the one police car approached us doormen, asked us if we saw anything strange going on that night. Asking us if we saw anything strange at that club was like asking the Pope at the Vatican if he had noticed anything religious going on! We all more or less replied the same,

"Nothing unusual, just a normal quiet night."

They went on to tell us they were going to have to leave the burger van where it was and forensics would come back later or in the morning. Any chance one of us could stay and keep an eye on the van until then? I explained I would have liked to but I had church in the morning. The other doorman gave their valid excuses as to why they couldn't help the police. No harsh feelings and off they went. As we approached our cars to drive off home, Rodney the Burger man and the Roid head appeared. They told us they had been hiding but watching it all happen from a distance, then asked us what had been said, so we told them.

"Right, thanks, lads, for not dropping me in it. Wait here two secs."

Ronald ran over to the burger van, went through the back door, came out with bags of frozen burgers and chips and gave them to us doormen. "Wait!" he said. He ran back to the van and came back with more food. He ended up giving us all the stock from his van.

"That's for you, lads. Get yourselves off; I've got a feeling this van is going to have a faulty gas line and explode once you're gone!"

Obvious what he meant so we cleared off. I arrived home and put my food in the freezer. Next morning, I took it down the local soup kitchen and gave it away; it's nice to be nice, but also, do you think the police are going to search a burnt-out burger van and find no food and not want to go talk to the last people seen there? No chance! I had done nothing wrong but I wasn't taking the chance. As for Ronald the burger man, he was lucky that night; nothing came of it. Later that year, he got arrested in Amsterdam, not sure what for; he probably had a mobile Cheese van or was selling tulips. The two lads from the rave were lucky; they went to court for public disorder, but only after 9 months of being on bail for intent to supply. I heard in court one of them said he couldn't cook so he had no intention of supplying burgers.

32.

Alsatian

One night on the door I was working this venue, an alright place, not much trouble. It was about the time most bars were getting extensions to midnight and 1 am, which was a bad thing, because by the time you finished those places, it was too late really to go to work a nightclub, so you were only getting the one wage for the night instead of two wages and the nice little scam that went with that. So, we were stood there greeting the punters, having a chat, keeping an eye on each other, or as they like to say in the doorman game 'watching each other's back'. I got chatting to a nice young lady, and chatting all the time, though not taking my eye off the game; that's what I'm paid for. Some doormen would talk to women and give them eye to eye contact longer than they should do, taking their eyes off the game. That used to do my nut how unprofessional they could be like that. So, I carried on chatting to this young lady and I got invited back to her house for a coffee when I finished work. I thought to myself, 'I fancy a bit of the old mellow bird' (young 'uns won't get that)! She was nice, pretty and well-kept, so at the end of the night we were getting close to closing time. The venue had eight people in with four doormen working. I told the other doorman I was going to sneak off, (so much for being professional, eh?)

Me and my new coffee-making friend got into my car and I asked her where she lived. She told me and we set off. I thought to myself, 'That's a nice area'. She'd already been telling me earlier on in the night what she did for a living and she had a lot going for her; good job, pretty, lived in a nice area, I was thinking she was going to have some top brand coffee in her gaff; might be a few bourbons on the go and some cheese on toast. Fuck me, she might even have some Worcester Sauce to go on top of the cheese on toast - even better! She was that classy she might have put some cucumber on as well. I was losing it; I'd gone into Homer Simpson donut mode over cheese on toast! 1 2 3 I was back in the car, and my friend didn't even realise I'd drifted off while she was waffling on.

We pulled up outside her house, got out the car and walked up the drive. As we got to the door, she pulled a bunch of keys out of her handbag and put a key inside the yale lock and turned it.

'WOOF', 'WOOF', fucking 'WOOF' came from inside the house. These were not ordinary 'WOOFS', these were big geezer dog 'WOOFS' and like the idiot I am, I said, "What's that?" Like she was going to turn round to me and say,

"Oh yeah, it's my cat!" The stupid things you come out with when you get nervous. She replied, "It's my dog". Now you know when they say an owner looks like her dog, I would expect this charming young lay to have a pink poodle or a fluffy, fluffy dog, if they exist, and inside, I was hoping she was going to tell me that was the kind of dog she had but it just had a deep tone to its 'WOOFS'. No such luck, she told me she owned an Alsatian. Now, I'm in a right dilemma; is it worth the risk of getting mauled while I'm trying to get mauled, if ya know what I mean? So, I decided, 'Fuck it I'm going in!' We entered the house; she stood in front of me, sort of guarding me from the incoming missile of teeth and fur. She bent down and outstretched her arms.

"Hello, my little beauty," she said, all squeaky-voiced, rubbing the underside of the beast. "Who's been a good boy, then? Has he missed Mummy?" All the time, the Alsatian's eyes were fixed on me. I was looking in another direction as I didn't want to make eye contact but I was aware of him sizing me up. So, eventually, she told me he was okay. "He won't bite you. He's very soft. Shall we go to the kitchen?" As we walk into the kitchen, I hear a squawk to my left side, and there is a bird in a cage. As the bird squawks, the dog barks; it's like something out of 'Ace Ventura: Pet Detective'. I was thinking I needed to get out of here before a monkey jumped out of a kitchen cupboard or a giraffe stuck its head through the kitchen window. I politely asked if I could use the toilet.

"Sure," she said, "there is one just through that doorway in front of you. I'll put the kettle on." I walked the length of the kitchen and opened the door, and there was a tiny room and another door in front of me leading to a toilet. I shut the door behind me, and at the same time, opened the other door in front of me, half expecting there to be a goldfish bowl in there. I relieved myself with a number 1, flushed the toilet, washed my hands, turned and opened the toilet door, stepped through, reached out and opened the door in front of me with my left hand as I shut the door behind me with my right hand. I stepped into the kitchen and straight away my spider senses started tingling that something wasn't right. There, straight in front of me, was the Alsatian, staring at me, viciously snarling. I smiled at the dog, trying to be friendly. He raised the noise of his snarls as if to tell me my smiles ain't going to save me. I said, in the softest voice I could muster up, "Excuse me, excuse me, could you get your dog, please?" No answer. The dog took a step forward; I smiled again at the mass of teeth and fur and said again, very softly, "Excuse me, excuse me, can you get your dog, please?" The dog took another step forward. Now I'm beginning to think I need the toilet again, but this time for a number 2! I was going to get ripped to shreds here. Just as I was about to break down in tears, there was a squawk from the bird on the kitchen side. The dog turned his head to look up at the bird, I jumped back through the doorway and slammed the door shut. As I did so, there was a thud against the door of the Alsatian having launched itself towards me. Now I was trying to compose myself, but I can't. My nervous energy was taking over.

"Oiiii!!! Fucking Oiiii!!!!" I started screaming. The dog started barking louder, the bird started squawking louder and the whole coffee thing has gone mad, never mind the cheese on toast bit. Where the fuck is she? I started thinking, 'What the fuck is going on? Is this some sort of sick game to make me the Alsatian's pedigree chum? I couldn't climb out the toilet window; it was too small and I'm not the leanest of people; to be honest, if you know me, you'll know I have a squeeze getting through patio doors. What the fuck am I going to do? I got my mobile phone out and rang one of the doormen I have been working with that night, knowing he wouldn't have gone straight home but would be having a coffee somewhere. He answered his phone, but before I could speak, he said,

"What the fuck is that noise?" I told him to "shut the fuck up and listen". I continued to tell him that I was in right limbo and I needed his help. I told him as quickly as I could what had happened and that the girl had disappeared. Do you know what he did? He started laughing and hung up on me! I was raging! I was so mad I nearly fancied my chances with the ferocious beast on the other side of the door. Then I heard the voice of my saviour; it was the young lady. She started shouting, "Get down, Rex!" I was thinking that must be short for T-Rex

"What you done to my baby?" I guessed that question was aimed at me. Now I wanted to explode all my anger on her after she asked such a stupid question, but I knew if I did that, I was not getting out of that house alive, so I replied, "I don't know. I came out of the toilet and your dog just started going mental. Can you put him in another room, please, so I can come out?"

"Okay" she replied, and I heard her say, "Come on, Rex." I heard the pitter patter of paws on the kitchen lino as they both left the kitchen. My lady friend came back into the kitchen; "You can come out now," she said. "It's because he doesn't know you and I wasn't here. He must have thought you were a burglar." I looked at her, astonished, and asked,

"Where were you?"

"Oh, upstairs slipping into something more comfortable, then my friend rang me on my mobile and asked how I was getting on so I got chatting; you know how it is."

I was still trying to keep calm. "Know how it is? I come back for coffee and I nearly end up getting savaged!" I didn't mention the cheese on toast; for some peculiar reason, I wasn't feeling hungry. With that, the bird squawked; that was it for me. I said "Listen, I gotta be getting off. I'll have a coffee with you some other time." She started pulling a face and said, "I didn't really invite you back for coffee. I wanted something else."

"I know that, but Rex has ruined the moment for me. I'm getting off." I started heading for the front door.

"You bastard!" she said and I heard a noise behind me and I knew what it was - she was opening the door were Rex was! I opened the door double-quick, I started to run through the short garden to my car and pressed the remote-control key fob to unlock my car doors as I heard the words, "Get him, Rex".

I got into my car and slammed the door as Rex slammed his big snarling teeth against my window, and all the time letting out a Jurassic Bark.

I pushed the button to wind down the electric window on my front passenger side and shouted at the young lady, "Are you right in the fucking head?"

She shouted back, "Obviously not because I ain't even got any coffee in the house!" She thought she had the last word being clever, so I shouted back, "Yeah, well I bet you ain't got no fucking bread or cheese either!" That fried her head. As I slowly drove off with Rex jumping up and down at the side of my car like he was on a fucking pogo stick, I shouted one last thing; "And you're barred, ya fucking loon, and so is Rex!" She was shouting some obscenities as I pressed the button to wind up my passenger side window. I couldn't make out what it was. I was feeling all lethargic from all the excitement and I needed a coffee.

33.

Rottweiler

One night on the door, I was working this venue, an alright place, steady trade, never much trouble. The gaffer of the venue approached the head doorman and said,

"I have just had the police on the phone, telling me they are expecting a lot of trouble tomorrow with the local football match going on. They have advised me not to open."

At this point, I was thinking to myself, 'That ain't going to happen; money-mad, this gaffer is, just like every other gaffer I've worked for.'

"So, I need doormen on tomorrow daytime, or else I will have to shut for the daytime trade. Can you sort it out for me because I won't be here," he continued to tell the head doorman in his best 'oh woe is me' voice.

The head doorman nodded his head in a positive attitude and told the gaffer he would sort it. He looked to me and asked me if I wanted to work a few hours the next day? "Yeah, sure," I told him. He wandered off around the venue and went and asked the other doormen if they fancied it. When he came back to me, he only needed 4 doormen to work one door around the back of the venue. To get there, people would have to walk through the car park giving us a lot of time to prepare if any big groups of lads from away approached the back door, so we could lock up or tell them from a distance they wouldn't be allowed in. He also explained to me that one of the doormen who was working with me had worked this venue for years and had done this routine many times before and had a unique way of working it. I was thinking to myself, 'How the fuck can you work the door in a unique way, fuckin' idiot?'

Next day at 11 am, I turned up at the venue, met two of the other doormen by the back door, and asked them where the doorman is with the 'unique way' of working the door. They both started laughing and told me he would be with us anytime now. As they finished telling me this, a white Astra van pulled into the car park. I saw the fourth doorman driving the car. He parked up and got out of his car then waved to us, smiling as he went to the back door of his van and opened it up. He reached in and out he pulls a Rottweiler; not just any Rottweiler, a fucking big Rottweiler! I knew straight away what this 'unique way' now was; I was shocked. The music from the Omen film was going through my head,

"What the fuck is going on?" I asked the other two doormen, "You've got to be fucking kidding me? You can't have a Rottweiler on the fucking door!" I told them in disbelief.

"Why not?" replied one of the two doormen, laughing.

I didn't know how to answer or what to say; my mind went blank, which most people would probably say wasn't unusual for me.

We started working the door and I was keeping a distance from the four-legged bouncer. He didn't like me, I could tell. He kept giving me smug dirty looks, challenging me, letting me know he was in charge, and I reckon the smug bastard knew Omen was still playing in my head. People were coming into the venue and giving the Rottweiler some strange looks.

"Come over here, he won't bite you," said the doorman who had hold of the beast.

"No, you're okay, I'll stay over here, out of his way," I said, trying not to catch the eye of the Rottweiler, because I knew he knew what I am saying,

One of the other doormen starts to explain a story to the doorman with the dog about some event that had happened in his life, and as he was explaining, he started waving his hands about. The dog rose and snapped at his hand with a growl. I jumped back, even though I was nowhere near them. The doorman who got bitten let out a yelp, and grabbed his bitten hand with his other hand, which are both now starting to show blood,

"For fuck sake, fuck this. I'm off," said the doorman and with that, he walked out the door and went off. As he was seen walking away, the other doorman stupidly walked up to the door to have a look to see where he had gone, and fuck me, the Rottweiler did the same to him; a little jump, snap of the jaws and a gruff growl. Fuck me, this doorman jumped back, grabbed his bitten hand with his uninjured hand and yelped as blood started to appear.

"Fuck this, I'm off!" he said, and he shuffled to the door and out he went. I was thinking to myself, 'Oh yeah, this is a fucking very 'unique way' of working the door this; we don't need to worry about the away fans coming in and smashing the venue up, we've got a dog going to do it', and I fucking knew the dog was thinking he was going to have me next.

Moments later, the local constabulary turned up at the back door doing a check to make sure everything was alright and that we had no trouble. As they approached the door. I could see the look on their faces of 'hello, hello, hello, what the fuck is all this then!' They started to talk to the doorman with the Rottweiler and asked him how everything was. I was thinking, 'I bet the dog doesn't bite the two bobbies, because he knows he'll be arrested'. Telling ya, this dog was smart. Not smart enough for me, though. I saw my chance to kill two birds with one stone. I shimmied past the doorman and the dog, and as I got outside, I started to whisper to the police about there being an assault in the venue that day by the security of the venue. They thought all their Christmases had come at once with Matty McCourt turning grass. I continued to tell them that the Rottweiler had bitten two other doormen, but they told me to fuck off, that I was having them on. I said, "No, honestly, it's the truth and the dog hasn't got an SIA badge; the dog is working illegally." I wanted to finish the sentence with 'ask him', but I thought I might be pushing my luck to get a result. (I had a mate once who used his dog as a witness to where he hadn't been one night, and when the Old Bill hassled him, he told the police to ask his dog. Their reply was "Okay, we will do." HONEST). The police walked back up to the doorman with the Rottweiler and asked him if the dog was a registered door supervisor. The doorman replied sarcastically,

"Of course, he is, officer. He can do first aid and give mouth to mouth. Bend down, ya fucking idiot, and he'll show ya"! The anger in the voice of the doorman made the Rottweiler get to his feet, which made the police take a step back in precaution, which made the Rottweiler sense fear, which made the doorman tighten his grip on his leash, which made me step back in fear that something was going to happen, which made the policeman shuffle another step back, which made the Rottweiler lean towards the police more, which made me think it's going to go off, which it did. Snarl, growl, bark, slaver all seemed to happen at the same time from the dog's jaws as it lunged towards the already retreating police. The doorman struggled to keep control. I was making off in another direction from the police. I could hear the two bitten, or should I say bitter, doormen laughing at the commotion. I started to run towards the bitten doormen who started to run off. I could hear the venue full of people cheering at what was going on. I was t to myself, 'This has massively backfired on me'. I kept running till I could manage to half turn my head and see that the Rottweiler was still going in the same direction as the police and the other two doormen were heading in a different direction to all of us. I stopped running and caught my breath. I started to hear the sounds of sirens in the distance, thinking to myself that it wouldn't surprise me if they were for the devil dog. How wrong was I? A couple of police vans appeared in the distance and drove straight to the venue we had run away from! Obviously, somebody in the venue had rung them. I started to run back to the venue, and as I ran through the car park, I was greeted by two police vans loaded with Old Bill, all dressed up in riot gear. They started to jump out of the vans and storm into the venue. People started leaving. I heard the police shouting, "Everybody leave now!!! Everybody out!" I approached a Robocop wannabe and asked what was going on. He told me they were under strict orders to shut the venue because there had been some trouble and two policemen had been assaulted. Also, the venue had been told to have doormen on today and as they arrived, there was no door security on.

Within five minutes, the venue was empty and the doors were shut. The bar staff were all moaning at me like it was my fault. There was a knock on the back doors; it was the two bitten doormen. I went to the door and let them in. They asked me what had happened, so I explained what Robocop had said to me.

"The gaffer is going to go mad; he could have made a mint today," replied the doorman, still holding his hand.

"Oh, really? Do you think so? He'll probably have to pay for the dog to do a door supervisor course if he doesn't bar him," I said, sarcastically, still trying to get my head around the day's events, when, in the background, I heard a gullible-sounding voice say, "Do you reckon?"

34.

Back Doors

One night on the door, I was working this venue, a good place to work it was in its heyday, very popular with locals and people from away. It was in a prime location and had good takings every day of the week. I worked with a good team of lads on the door. I liked working there; the pay wasn't the best. I had been there for about two years, on and off, but was also working other places that paid better money. Because it was brewery-owned and the gaffer of the pub was on a bonus system, we would never get a free drink at the end of the night. We had a kitty between the doormen which we put into every week to buy teabags, coffee and sugar. I mean, the gaffer was that tight to get his bonus pay he wouldn't let us use the sugar; we had to buy that ourselves. The gaffer was a Flash Harry cunt. He had a girlfriend much younger than him, but she was only into him because he'd give her free drinks. She was as flirty as him with the punters. He was one of these gaffers who thought he was good-looking, thought he was hard as fuck, he thought he was a millionaire, he thought he was the new Peter Stringfellow, he thought he was clever; he thought fucking wrong then, didn't he? Now this venue had three points of entrance, and the doormen used to have two on each door. The front door was busy controlling the queues to get in, but the side door was easy to work; that was always kept closed and was just a fire exit or, if needs be, a convenient place to exit undesirables. The back door was a fairly easy number - it led onto the patio area; this was in the days before the smoking ban so there was never any need for anybody to go on to the patio. It was supposed to be the same as the side door, more of a fire exit, but if you had a mate turn up at the back door to avoid the queue, you would let them in discreetly. Now, you know how the mind works; you tell your mate to come to the back door and be discreet and you would let him in, but, partly because of the alcohol and partly to look like some kind of celeb, he turns up with every man and his fucking dog to get in the back door. Then, before you know it, word gets around and now you're getting a queue at the back door nearly as long as the queue at the front door trying to get in. By the way, you didn't have to pay to enter this venue, it was free; I think people just had a thing about back door entry. So, by offering to do your mates a favour, it had backfired and now we had created a monster of unnecessary grief! Now, on the back door, we were having to tell people they couldn't come in. What made all of this situation worse was that there was no handle on the inside of the door to pull it shut, but there was a handle on the outside of the door. Fuck knows who decided that when designing the doors! We used to tell Flash Harry to have a handle placed on the inside of the doors to make it easy to pull them shut, but he wasn't interested.

Another thing that used to happen, which I found quite disturbing, was the number of sexual favours you got offered by women just so you would let them in the back door. Unbelievable! I kid you not, I remember one night working the back door and I was offered a sexual favour by a nice, very attractive girl who was part of a group of girls. I refused in a polite way but I was disgusted. What made that situation worse was that after some polite chat to get them to go away, I found out who she was, and who her fiancé was and that at that time, I was playing Saturday afternoon football with him! Big no-no for me; millions of girls in the world so why ruin a friendship by going with a friend's girl?

So, this Friday night, it was wintertime and I was working the back door of the venue. It was not a very busy night in the venue or around the area, no queues at the front door, and still, people came round to the back door because they liked the buzz of getting in like some kind of celeb. I politely told people to go round to the front door. Now, three girls started walking up to the back door. All three of them were very inebriated (pissed as farts), so I told them they couldn't come in the back door. They ignored me and carried on walking forward. Once again, I told them they couldn't come in the back door, but they carried on ignoring me, drunkenly chatting amongst themselves. Once they reached the back door, again I told them they would have to go round to the front door. Now, one of the girls offered a sexual favour. It wasn't a real offer, it was a 'YOU'RE A THICK AS FUCK DOORMAN WHO WILL SAY YES BECAUSE I AM GORGEOUS AND A CLASS ABOVE YOU, CRETIN'! Yep, I read all that in the few words she said. Not a chance now were they coming in for trying to mug me off. I despised the punters that judged doormen as being stupid and beneath them, so there was no way they were getting in my back door, not even if they encouraged me to get in their back door; not a chance! The girl who had offered me the sexual favour tried to push me out the way and told me that I wasn't going to stop her from entering through my back door. I place my hand on her shoulder and told her not to push me. As I did so, she collapsed to the floor on her knees like some kind of balloon just emptied of all its air. That was it! Her two clueless mates went on the warpath. "You've just hit her!" one of them screamed.

"No, I haven't, trust me, if I had hit her she wouldn't be sat on her knees in front of me, she'd be lying flat about 10 feet away!" I replied.

Her response to that was, "Well, if you just let us in your back door, we'll forget about it."

Yep, so I've allegedly assaulted her and they will forget about it if I let them in my back door? It ain't happening.

Now they wanted to see the gaffer, Flash Harry, I told my partner to get the gaffer. He appeared and, straight away, he was flirting with the girls. He took them out of earshot of me. I could see the girl who offered to forget about things waving her arms about, her mouth waffling on like she was on speed. The gaffer was looking at her, nodding in agreement. I knew he was not taking in any of what she was saying - he was just thinking about getting into her knickers! Then, right at the end of her arm-waving and rapid mouth movement, she did the motion of a slam dunk you see in wrestling, so now I knew that she'd been telling the gaffer that I had assaulted her friend. Fuck me, by her actions I more than assaulted her, I had a WWF wrestling match with her!

The gaffer turned away from the girl, walked towards me with the three girls following and said, "Let them in the back door." I was fucking raging.

"Okay, I'll let them in but just let me tell you this; whatever she just said to you is all bollocks. That girl collapsed to the floor pissed up."

"I know that! I know you're not that kind of person," he replied with a big fucking cheesy grin on his face. "Just let them in as a favour to me. I know them!"

Lying bastard - he didn't know them, but I let them in. So now, I have to watch him at the bar entertaining the three girls, obviously slagging me off by the actions of them laughing, looking over at me and laughing again. At the end of the night, I went through the motions of finishing my shift and could not wait to get out of there.

Next morning, the head doorman rang me on my mobile phone to tell me that Flash Harry didn't want me working on his door after I had assaulted the women last night and that he'd had to talk the girls out of going to the police. I told the head doorman exactly what had happened. I told him the other doormen would back my story up and so would the CCTV. I also told the head doorman that, in a way, I was glad because I didn't want to work for Flash Harry. I said I had no problems with him, the doorman, and that he was an excellent head doorman who I had learned a lot from. I wished him well and hung up the phone. I wasn't happy; I was far from happy. I needed to enforce 'Lex Talionis'!

So, I waited for a couple of weeks. I found out that Flash Harry was away for the weekend, so I called into the venue on a Friday night after finishing working at another venue. I chatted to the doorman there and had a laugh, all the time doing my recce. I left and went and sat in my car in the car park and did an outside recce. Next night, after I finished work at the place I was working, we had a staff drink. I told the staff I was just nipping off to the toilet. Down the corridor was a motion sensor on the wall, not very high. I place a layer of

Sellotape over the sensor; the tape was invisible once stuck down. Now a motion sensor works like this; if there is motion, a red light at the side lights up, and if there is no motion, the red light doesn't come on. You probably all know this - it's the same system as your basic house alarm. I went to the toilet and when I came out into the hallway in range of the motion sensor, no light came on. I removed the tape and returned to finish my staff drink.

I then went to the venue managed by Flash Harry. On the way, I picked up my friend; we shall call him Raffles. Now, me and Raffles go back to school days. We were from the same estate. I entered the venue on my own. "Hey, two nights on the trot!" shouted one of the doormen. "Yeah, I love it here!" I shouted back. I stood at the bar opposite the back door, bought myself an orange juice because I was driving, and got Raffles a bottle of Budweiser. I showed Raffles the motion sensor that covered that part of the bar and the back door, then we waited until closing time. None of the doormen were bothering us to rush our drinks, so I walked around the area between the back door and the bar, roughly 20 feet square, before another motion sensor red light would flash showing it had picked you up.

So here was the plan.

Raffles would 'smash the back doors' open; didn't matter about the alarm going off, he was going in there to place Sellotape over the motion sensor by the back door, so he would be in and out in seconds. Obviously, the gaffer would come downstairs, the police would arrive, the usual process of checking the bar would happen, then the police would search the immediate area. They'd all be happy nothing was taken.

Flash Harry would be smug with the police and tell them that the venue's safe was at the other end of the building behind two locked doors and that the safe was the Ray Winstone (Daddy) of safes; you would need dynamite to get in there.

The next night after work, I called into the venue for a quick beer on the way home. I stood at the end of the bar by the back door. The place was quiet; every time I moved along the bar, out of the corner of my eye, I was looking for a red light to flash; it never happened. I texted my friend Raffles and told him I would have to cancel our croquet appointment as I was going out of town for the night. That night, I heard somebody had 'smashed the back doors' of that venue again and had taken the ATM machine, taken the cigarette machine and ironically, the bandits had taken the bandit! Nobody could work out how they had done it so quickly - obviously an inside job and Flash Harry must have been involved! Apparently, he was given a right grilling by the brewery and taken in for questioning by the police. Less than two weeks later, he had left the venue and his girlfriend had left him. It turned out, through all the investigations, that they had caught Flash Harry fiddling the books and till receipts. Shame, that. You see, he was that concerned with thinking that the safe was the target, without realising the real reason for having his 'Back Doors Smashed In'.

35.

Scrumping

One night on the door, I was working this venue, a nightclub which was always busy, but most of the time, busy for the wrong reasons. There was a lot of trouble in this place. It wasn't a regular place for me, it was just handy that most of the time when I finished working other venues close by, this place was open later so the head doorman there would come and see me if he was short of staff and ask me if I would come and do a bit to help him out. No problem; I was already out working in my monkey suit, so it was nice to get a little bit of extra cash on top of what I was earning after just buying my first house. This venue had lads working the door there from all different sorts of backgrounds, all very handy. You had your judo men, boxers, strong men, karate men and your 'I'm a fuckin loony' men. To be fair, though, just to work there you had to be not right in the head. The other venues close by were the same as this place for employing doormen of the loony kind; that was the kind of area where these venues were situated. All the doormen at all these different venues knew each other through one way or another; work, crime, business, needlework class, you know the kind of thing, and the doormen working the other venues used to nearly always visit the late-night venue after their places had closed for few extra drinks, a bit of business or perhaps to sort out needlework class designs.

So, this one night, as I was working the late-night venue, the lads who I had been working with earlier on at another venue turned up. They came into the foyer and it just kicked off between all the doormen. I didn't have a clue what was going on, I was just doing my best to try and stop everybody fighting each other. I had no chance; it was like pissing in the wind! Eventually, it calmed down. Everybody started shaking hands, apologising and laughing with each other, and I just stood there thinking, 'What the fuck has just happened? Are this lot for real?' The visiting doormen headed in towards the main part of the venue. I leant towards one of the doormen who was working the late-night venue and asked him what was going on. He leant back towards my direction and whispered to me, "Fucked if I know, I just got stuck in!" then leant back away from me, back to his original stance, stood up straight. So, I then leant back towards him and whispered "See if you can find out, will you?" and then I leant back away from him, back to my original stance, stood up straight. He looked back towards me and I was thinking to myself, 'I hope that he doesn't lean back towards me because this is getting stupid now. I feel like I am in a Michael Jackson video'.

The end of the night was upon us and I was still none the wiser to what the fight in the foyer was about. I hadn't had the chance to ask the doormen from either venue as I had been busy all night dealing with bits and bobs, tits and knobs, which was the norm for this late-night venue. Eventually, the last customer of the night left and we settled down for our customary late-night staff free drink. The doormen from the other venue joined us and we all start chatting about the usual macho boring shit. I was still thinking to myself, 'I have no idea what that fight was about earlier on', then one of the doormen suggests going down the street to a house which has an apple tree in its front garden and scrumping some apples, to which all the doormen apart from me laughed and then agreed.

So, here was the situation I was in; earlier in the night, two sets of doormen from different venues had a fight between each other for a reason I don't know, and now they were agreeing to team up and go rape an apple tree in somebody's front garden! Never in that short time of me doing the door had I seen anything so weird as this, but I thought to myself, 'Fuck it, I'll go along and get myself some apples. My missus is a decent cook; does a nice apple pie; in for a dollar in for a Granny Smith'. So, we finished our drinks and left the venue, all 12 of us dressed in black suits and dickie bows, some of us pissed, some sober, walking down the street trying to be quiet; no chance of that happening! One of the drunken doormen offered to climb the tree and chuck the apples down for everybody to collect; he told everybody he was really agile and could climb anything. I never said anything but all I was thinking was, 'The fat bastard couldn't climb into bed unless there was a jam doughnut laid there in lingerie'! So, fat Spiderman scaled the wall and jumped to the tree; to be fair, quite impressive even with the pause for an alcoholic belch. He started to chuck the apples from the tree and we started to pick them up and put them in our pockets because nobody had the brains to bring any bags, and If they had of brought bags, we could have got all our potential bootleg cider back to the venue five minutes away and evenly dished out all the apples between one another, rather than get into the farce which was just about to happen.

211

So, fat Spiderman dropped a couple more apples which two doormen leapt forward to pick up. The only thing was, it is one doorman from each different crew, so the 'ALPHA MALE' bit kicked in. The doorman from the late-night venue crew ended up getting three apples to the doorman from the earlier venue crew's one apple. I thought to myself, 'Great.' I already knew what was going to happen, so of course they started arguing about sharing the apples two apiece, then the other doormen from both sides got involved. There was a lot of arguing and raised voices, then lights from the various houses around us started to come on due to the noise. The raised voices changed to pushing and shoving, then grabbing, then the first punch was thrown followed by more punches from both crews. There were men on the floor wrestling, apples getting strewn all over the place, more lights coming on around the area, doors and windows began to open from nearby houses and people were shouting, adding to the noise. I couldn't make out what they were shouting but I had a good idea it would be to keep the noise down, which was quite ironic because they were adding to the noise! Then, in the distance, at the end of the street, the blue lights of a police van appeared, then came blue lights from the other end of the street. I couldn't make out if it was a police van or car, but could see it was travelling at speed, so I thought to myself, 'I'm out of here quicker than a Pink Lady on a Scrumpy Jack diet! I knew to head towards the police van then take the side street because they were going to see me but not stop. They would just keep heading towards all the commotion of the lads. I decided to leave my car until the morning; I just needed to get out of the area, but I was still in two minds whether to dump my apples. I didn't want to get done for theft, but I did like my wife at the time's apple pies; she was an exceedingly good cook (yeah, I put cook).

I made it to the side street. The police van drove past and the police did look at me but didn't stop, as I predicted. As I came out the other end of the short side street to a crossroads, in front of me, I could see more blue lights approaching. I needed to hide or get a taxi; I didn't fancy a night in the cells, and as luck would have it, a taxi appeared from another street to the left of me. I flagged it down, it stopped and I jumped into the back seat and I gave the taxi driver an address in the street next to mine. I would run through the alleyway to get to my house (never get a taxi driver to drop you off at your home address if you're in the area of something naughty!) I tried not to speak to him, just kept yawning. We pulled up outside the address I had given him, and as I went to pay him, he laughed and said,

"Cheers, Matty!" Waste of time, all that then! As he pulled off, I ran down the alleyway into the street where I lived and got home safe and sound with my six apples.

Next morning, I was up early after only a few hours' sleep. I decided to walk to get my car as it was a nice fresh Sunday morning and leave the missus to start baking my apple pie. No good; she told me she needed more apples. Always fucking moaning; moaned if she never had anything to moan about! I told her I would be back with some more apples. I wanted to get her a special red apple from that Snow White's step mum...

I got to my car and decided to have a drive past where all the insanity had gone on earlier that morning. I couldn't believe it; the police had it taped off! Now I was panicking, wondering if somebody had been stabbed, somebody seriously hurt. I didn't want to get on my mobile phone and start ringing round. More serious than that, though, I had to now go and buy some apples from the shop to keep her indoors happy to finish off my apple pie.

I visited a doorman's house to see what had gone on. He started laughing and explained to me that the house with the apple tree belonged to some kind of solicitor, barrister or legal eagle of some kind, and that when the police got there, they were not too bad dealing with the situation and were probably going to let everybody get on their merry way, but the owner of the house came out and started reciting laws and numbers and that he was a freemason and something else they should all be afraid of and wanted everybody arrested and charged, so everybody started arguing. He lost count of how many police turned up. Some bigwig chief of police turned up and decided anybody found in possession of apples was going to the cells but the cells were full up, it was a Saturday night. So, then he wanted the names and address of everybody there for further enquiries and ongoing investigations into a possible breach of the peace

Next day, I got a visit from the police to my house. I was at my daytime job. When my wife rang me to tell me, I told her I hoped she hadn't let them in, because if they'd found the apple pie, they would have seized it for evidence! I started laughing to myself, thinking she would be freaking out now, moaning that the police were going to take away her baking. Besides that, I had a receipt for the apples from the shop and I would be on CCTV buying them, so unless they did a CSI into how many apples make up a pie the size of hers, I was in the clear.

36.

You Pay for What You Get

One night on the door, I was working this venue, a lovely place; it was more of a restaurant with a few drinkers frequenting the place; a right easy number off the beaten track. I worked there for six years as well as other places at the same time. At that time, I was running five venues, pubs, clubs and restaurants and I had 19 lads working for me on a Saturday night, but the SIA soon put a stop to all that. Anyway, in the six years of running the door at this restaurant, we never had one fight. Obviously, we had a few things to deal with but nothing to shout about. After six years, the guy who owned the place was looking to lease it out, so a new owner came in and took over and straight away h was laying down the law, telling us we were going to have to take a pay cut with no free cups of coffee and no free food. So, I told the bloke, "No problem, I won't be staying. I'll work one more weekend for you and you can get one of the local door agencies in," which was always going to be his plan. I knew of the new owner and I knew he was pally with one of the owners of a local doorman agency. I didn't give a fuck; I was off! Let him pay shit money and get himself a shirt-filler.

The last weekend I worked there, on the Friday night, I went into the kitchen as I usually did and had a chat with the head chef. He always cooked me some kind of tasty snack. He was good at his job, in high demand. He started telling me the new owner told him he had to take a pay cut and demanded some other stupid cost-cutting ideas, so the chef had told him he was going and it was his last weekend. So that was it; we were both leaving the next night.

Now, do you ever get that feeling when you are looking at someone that you both start thinking the same thing? Well, that's what happened. In that split second of looking at each other, we were both thinking we were going to leave this place with some sort of compensation. All I did was give him the nod and say, "I'll sort it for tomorrow night."

"Okay," he replied with a big cheesy smirk.

So, the next night, I turned up for work. I nipped into the kitchen, looked at the chef, and he just said, "It's all good to go!"

"Nice one," I said, heading for the cellar full of all the booze and freezers of food. In case you are wondering, in the pub game you still say cellar referring to where you store your supplies, even though most of the new places store their supplies on the ground floor because they don't have a cellar, as was the case with this place.

The new owner was in the restaurant giving it Bertie Big Bollocks, like some kind of Peter Stringfellow. He didn't really speak to me that night, which suited me.

I got one of the lads who was working for me at another venue to turn up at the back of the restaurant in a van, and as he pulled up, I give him the nod. He jumped out and followed me into the cellar (supply room). We started grabbing bottles of wine and then pulling the ones from the back to the front of the shelf, so it looked like nothing had been taken. We placed them carefully in the back of his van, rushed back in, took a couple of cases of the bottled beer each, then went back in -

well, you get the idea! Then the chef appeared and said, "Quick! Take the food!" I never gave it a thought to take the food, so now we were grabbing frozen items of food out the freezers; fuck knows what they were but we were having it! Right, van loaded, we got the van the fuck out of there. I walked back through the kitchen and looked at the chef. He looked at me then looked away. I walked back into the restaurant and through the diners and made my way to the door to stand back with my partner.

"Everything go okay?" he said quietly, hardly moving his lips.

"Sweet as," I replied quietly, trying not to move my lips. "Did the new gaffer ask where I was?" I whispered again, looking in the opposite direction to my partner but still with stiffened lips.

"Yeah, he came and asked where you were and I told him you had gone for a shit in the disabled toilet," my partner whispered back, but I could tell he was doing it without moving his mouth. I turned my head and looked at him and replied, "We got plenty of gottles of geer, gottles of geer!" Well, that was it! We both cracked up laughing and he told me that night I could be Lord Charles and he would be Roger De Courcey, so as people were entering the venue that mighty fine evening, we were opening the door for them and saying, "Good evening," with not one muscle movement of the face.

About 15 minutes after my friend had cleared off in his van, he rang me on my mobile phone.

"What am I going to do with all the rest of this food? My freezer is full and so is the mother-in-law's freezer and my brother's freezer!"

He was telling me this down the phone in a panicky voice like we'd just committed the crime of the century and were going to be on next month's Crimewatch.

"For fuck sake, man, chill the fuck out! Take the rest of the food down the homeless centre and give them it as a donation from the restaurant. Just don't let them see your van reg. As for the booze, we will divvy (divvy in this case meaning share) that up later."

When we finished our shift at the end of the night, nothing was mentioned; nobody had noticed any difference to the cellar. Nice one; job's a good 'un. I shook the new gaffer's hand as we left, wished him all the best and he wished me all the best. Neither of us meant it, and we both knew that we both didn't mean what we both just said, which made our illegal takeaway even sweeter.

A couple of days later, I met up with the chef and squared him up with his share. In the local paper that night, the owner of the restaurant had a write up about how he had made a donation of food to the local homeless centre and how the centre was overwhelmed with his generous donation of top-quality food. He didn't last long at the venue, neither did the next owner or the owner after that. It eventually closed and reopened as a Thai restaurant and then closed again. I like to think that the reason for the failure of the place after me and my partner leaving was just that; the opening of the door as people walked into the restaurant, the way we talked to people, the offer to ring taxis for the customers as they were about to leave, the professionalism of standing on the door looking very smart, smelling nice and interacting, rather than the doormen that followed us who were shirt-fillers, smoking on cigars. I mean, for fuck sake, cigars stink! They were dressed like shit, not opening the doors for customers, not offering to ring a taxi. Don't get me wrong, there would be a job for them somewhere to work the door, just not that kind of venue. As the saying goes, you pay for what you get.

37.

Snoring Straightener

One night on the door, I was working this venue; it was probably the best place I worked. It was mad, it was crazy, it was popular, the music was great; the wages we got paid were very good for that era, but we earned it. There was never a quiet night and never a dull moment, NEVER. This particular night, at the beginning of the shift, we had a crew of local lads turn up. All of the doormen working knew them. I knew one of them very well because he and his brother used to do karate with me some years before. Now, I ain't no psychologist and I don't think any of the other doormen were, but you get to learn body language working the doors, and by their body language, you could tell these lads weren't coming up to the club to dance the night away; they were in the club on business and we all knew it. I suppose you could say we should have stopped them from coming in the door, but that crew of lads I worked with there, we didn't give a fuck. It was a hard crew, mentally and physically hard, all well-known in their chosen sporting combat activities as well as being well-known for their street activities. This was in the days before the SIA badges came in; old-school doormen who didn't like dealing with the police, because most of the time they were dealing with the police. A mix of people continued to enter the venue and then another crew of lads turned up. Myself and the other doormen knew without knowing that they were coming in for trouble and we knew it was going to be with the other crew of lads who had entered earlier. Again, you would be right to think we should have stopped them at the door and not let them in; me, personally, I always wanted quiet nights on the door, I wanted money for nothing and the chicks for free, but the other doormen working with me didn't give a fuck, and like I say, that set of doormen was very confident in their abilities on the door and whatever afters entailed after we finished working the door. This meant that with these particular doormen, if you crossed them, it didn't just finish on the door, they would find you, if not that night, they would find you and serve retribution later. The second crew of lads was also known to us on friendly terms and one of their crew was a martial artist and trained with one of the doormen who worked with us.

So, sure enough, after about half an hour of the second crew of lads entering, we had a call to go to the back room because there was a situation. The full set of doormen attended, to be confronted by both crews of lads in a stand-off, waving hands at each other, shouting and making 'come on, let's fight' gestures. Now, if this went off, it was going to get very messy. The head doorman told both sets of lads to calm down, then said, "Whatever your beef is, take it outside and settle it, or even better, have your main man from each crew have a straightener to settle the difference." None of us doormen knew what the problem was between the two crews of lads, we just presumed it would be down to a drug deal gone wrong. Both crews of lads agreed and we started heading towards the fire exit. Outside the venue, across the road, was an old car park with a barrier across the entrance stopping cars from entering (don't ask). The car park was sheltered on either side by tall old warehouses, a perfect place for a straightener.

As we all entered the car park, it had already been decided who from each crew was going to represent them, and each crew had chosen the lads who both did karate. I looked over at the doorman who trained with the other lad and we both smiled at each other because now it was more than a straightener between these two crews of lads; now it was about which karate style would come out on top or who was going to have the bragging rights between me and my doorman friend. My doorman friend who trained in martial arts, I had nothing but respect for. He trained in Shotokan Karate, while I trained in Wado Ryu. He was a very deep martial artist, he trained all the time, he trained with good lads from my area and he had also trained all over the country with some of the very best martial artists in the land. He had been on seminars with grandmasters; I think, at that time, the only thing he hadn't done was go to Japan. My background, compared to his, was that I trained hard, read books and did a few competitions, the odd nunchuka course and a few seminars with guys who were high up in my Association, but no masters from the old country, though.

We formed a sort of human circle in the car park as the two lads squared up. No messing about between the two of them, they went for it; fast kicks and punches with good technique coming from both of them. They got into a clinch and both head-locked each other as they both bent, still with their free hand both throwing punches, they fell backwards to the ground. I think this move happened because they both made the move to sweep the legs away from the other. They continued on the floor trying to beat each other, while all the time, the human ring around them was closing in and shouting for their man to beat the shit out of the other man. Now, this was real life, not a choreographed movie fight scene. Fights in real life last seconds that seem like hours if you're the one fighting, so eventually, both our gladiators were running out of steam. The moves on the floor were becoming slower and stagnated, so myself and my martial artist doorman friend pulled them apart. I grabbed the lad from my Karate Dojo and he grabbed his. They were both bloodied and bruised and had designer clothes ripped all over, but they had given a good account of themselves and everybody from both sides knew they had without saying anything. But still, there was tension in the air between both crews. We all started to walk out of the car park and as we did, somebody from the first crew tried to take a sly punch at the gladiator who had represented the other crew, but before his punch could land, my doorman martial artist friend had slipped under his arm, moved round the back of him, placed his arms in a position that locked his head and put him to sleep, then lowered him so gently to the floor. It was so fast and so impressive and took the tension up another notch. Now, we were in a Mexican standoff; there was crew number one and crew number two looking at us doormen, but there was no way they were going to join forces to take us on. It was just going to end up a free-for-all; the only thing missing now was the spaghetti western music. All it was going to take was for someone to make a move and it was all going to go off.

Then, out of nowhere came the sweet sound of peace, the sound that relieved all the tension, the sound that turned snarls and aggressive faces into smiling faces that led to faces full of laughter. Our friend on the floor, who had been put to sleep, had started snoring! The gentle sound of his snoring relieved the tension, and as his snoring got louder, so did the giggles and the laughing amongst us all. The tension was gone! Somebody reached down and grabbed Sleeping Beauty by his shoulder and gave him a shake.

"Wake up, wake up, you fuckin' div," he said, laughing. He turned around and looked at us all laughing, rolled his eyes, then turned to Sleeping Beauty and tugged his shoulder again. This time, the snoring stopped and he gave out a slight moan, which, in turn, brought on our laughter louder and stronger. Sleeping Beauty now opened his eyes and asked, "What the fuck is going on? Where am I?" The laughing continued. Sleeping Beauty rose to his feet and looked at us all.

"What you all laughing at?" he asked.

"Shall we get a drink?" said one of the gladiators to the other gladiator.

"Will we be allowed in?" he replied. They both looked in the direction of the head doorman, who looked at his crew of doormen for some help in his decision, rubbed his finger along his chin while deep in thought, looked at the gladiators and asked them,

"You going to be any trouble if we let you back in?"

"No," they replied simultaneously.

"Go on, then," said the head doorman, "and take Sleeping Beauty with you!"

They all returned to the club, spent the rest of the night all drinking and laughing together, then they all left together and went on to some house party, which was always the norm from this venue.

And that was that; we never bothered finding out what the beef was between the two crews; we weren't interested, to be honest. All I know is whenever I hear that saying, 'that's easy, I can do that in my sleep', I think of the time a potential bloodbath was stopped by someone in his sleep.

38.

Racist Doorman

One night on the door, I was working this place; a nice little number, no grief, just the two of us working the door. (This was in the days before Facebook and camera phones). We had a group of youngsters turn up a bit drunk. Now, if I was ever working a nice place, like the one I was at that night, where the vast majority of punters were older people who liked the company of other older people and were away from the boom, boom music, when it came to ID'ing someone, I wouldn't let them unless they were over 20. Now, you probably think that's out of order but on the flipside to that, when I worked other places and let's say the crowd were younger, if I were to ID someone and they pulled out ID showing they were a member of the forces, I never bothered checking it. If they were old enough to defend my country, then as far as I was concerned, they were old enough to come into the venue and drink alcohol.

So, I began to ID the youngsters. Two of them were borderline, just turned 18, one of them was 26, (yeah right); if he was 26, he was fuckin Peter Pan! It was obviously his brother's ID. The other three in the party were being dealt with by my partner. He looked at me, then turned to the 'Inbetweeners' and said, "not tonight, sorry". And so started the barrage of abuse. I'd heard it all before like all doormen have. They started making a scene; the boys wanted to fight us telling us how hard they were and that they were cage fighters;

more like cage makers, because they were being held back by their 7-stone, slim, no muscle girlfriends. They went on to tell us they knew all the local national and international gangsters, (see what happens when you have a day watching Sopranos?) While all this was going on, a police car passed by, got to the end of the street, turned round and came back to where we were and parked up. Two police officers got out of their car and in true 'Dixon of Dock Green' fashion, said, "Hello, hello, hello, what's all this then?" I think they were doing It for a piss-take because, as they said it, one of the officers bent his knees. My partner went to explain to one of the police officers what had gone on, while the other police officer was dealing with the 'Inbetweeners'. I couldn't hear what was being said by anybody as they had all moved a distance from the door in different directions. After a few minutes, the police officer who had been talking to the "inbetweeners" walked up towards the other police officer. As he got near, he reached his hand towards his belt, unbuckled a pair of handcuffs and slapped one end of them onto my partner. He then went to reach for my partner's other hand, but my partner pulled his arm away. He was in shock after the first handcuff being slapped on his wrist!

"What the fuck are you doing?" asked my doorman partner.

"You're under arrest," replied the officer. Funny how whenever a police officer says, 'you are under arrest', it sounds like they say it in a Gestapo voice! (I bet you now read that again in a Gestapo voice).

"What for?" asked my doorman partner.

"An alleged racist comment; you don't have to say anything, but anything you do say can and blah blah blah…" replied the police officer.

I couldn't believe what I was hearing, and by the look on my doorman partner's face, neither could he! I looked over at the 'inbetweeners'. They were all the same colour as me and my partner, which was white; well, I was a bit orangey - I'd had some free use of a sunbed.

"How the fuck can he be arrested for making racist comments," I shouted at the police officer, "when we're all the same fucking colour?"

"Watch your language, sir, or you will be arrested for swearing in a public place," replied the officer, walking my doorman partner to his patrol car. My partner looked back at me over his shoulder with a big smug smile. I knew what he was smiling for, but the whole situation was raging me now. The police had taken the word of some drunken teenagers as truth, without even questioning us sober professional doormen.

"Honestly, you guys are making a big mistake; huge!" I said to the police.

"Is that right? Are you threatening us, McCourt?" said the officer who wasn't dealing with my partner, as he walked up to me and stood square on to me.

"No, I'm not threatening you, I don't make threats," I replied taking a step into his personal space. "You misunderstood what I was trying to tell you, but seeing as though you think you know everything, I'll let you find out for yourself."

The police car pulled away with one officer driving and the other sat in the back next to my partner. The 'Inbetweeners' cleared off sharpish once the police car had pulled away, so I continued to work the rest of the night by myself. The manager of the venue had not seen what happened and, at the end of the night when we were closing, he asked me where my partner was. I told him he had just this second left, as he'd had a phone call from his wife to rush home.

"Oh, okay, I hope everything is okay." He was a good manager to work for; he just left us to our job. Not only that, he was a nice guy. I used to like having a chat with him after work while having our staff drinks. To tell you the truth, I didn't know anybody who didn't like him.

The next morning, my doorman partner rang me and told me what had happened down at the police station. He said that the 'inbetweeners' claimed he had made a racial slur towards them. When the police took him for interview, he refused to speak. He told me he didn't even say 'no comment'. While in the charge room collecting his belongings before being released, in front of the desk sergeant, the duty solicitor, the two arresting police officers and two further police officers, he said, "I don't think this will stand up in court. I can't see the Crown Prosecution Service pursuing this one." He told me that the fat desk sergeant said, "Really? Is that right? You're an expert in law, now, are you?"

"No," my partner replied, "but my missus will be soon once she passes out of law school. I only do this door work as well as my daytime job to support us both and our children until she passes. She would never have got this opportunity where she was from; Nigeria." We both started laughing; he continued to tell me that the best part of it all was that when they released him, they had to take him to the front reception of the police station, and as they opened the door, his missus was there to greet him. He said the look on the officers' faces was unforgettable; even the duty solicitor took great joy in the whole set-up, telling the officers he would love to be a fly on the wall when their superiors found out about this. A few weeks later, my doorman partner received a letter through the post from the Crown Prosecution Service saying all charges would be dropped.

Like I told the police, I don't make threats, and they were making a big mistake.

39.

Taxi Driver

One night on the door, I was working this venue, an alright place on the main drag amongst a load of bars and clubs, restaurants and takeaways. It was always busy and it was my first place as a head doorman. I had a good partner with me; we had worked together as partners for about 6 years and took on a lot of venues together. He was a good boxer, hard and loyal. He got on well and was liked by everybody; always laughing, hyper, never suffered fools. All of a sudden, he turned round to me one night and told me he'd had enough of working the door and that he was jacking it in to go taxi-driving. I couldn't believe what I was hearing! At that time, there was a surge of lads jacking in the door and going taxi-driving. Even some old-school doormen had done this and one of them sometimes used to pull up outside different venues and be telling doormen what a good screw they were on and that it was better money than working the door, so obviously, as with most things in life, money talks, so a few lads left working the doors and gave taxi-driving a go. It wasn't for me; hi diddly dee, a doorman's life for me.

So, my ex-doorman partner used to drive past some nights as I was stood on the door, toot his horn and give me a wave. On the odd occasion, he would pull over for a quick word, tell me the taxi-driving was alright and had its perks but was not as good as all the ex-doormen made out it was.

One night on the door, I was getting some grief from a Hooray Henry sort of geezer, you know the kind, looked down his nose at everybody, thought anybody with a penny less than him was a peasant, dressed like a bag of potatoes but liked to talk loud and let everybody in the venue know about his financial matters. He was drunk and the manager wanted him to leave, so eventually, we managed to talk him out the door; no physical contact; maybe took a few minutes more to get him out, but better than being physical when there is no need to be. It was never my style, that; my last resort was getting physical with punters. So now, Hooray Henry was stood outside the venue making threats, telling us he was going to buy the place and sack all the doormen, shouting and telling us we were useless and that he had more money than us, blah, blah, blah, nothing new, nothing original, nothing changes; then after all that, he asked me if I could ring him a taxi!

"Yeah, sure, no problem," I told him, and that was nothing out the ordinary. I would always do that if asked, the reason being that it got them away from the venue and away from the risk of there being any more confrontation. Just as I had replied to him, my ex-doorman partner drove past. I waved my hand at him and beckoned him to come back but he drove out of sight. Seconds later, my mobile phone, which was inside my Crombie coat, began to ring. I answered my phone and it was my ex-doorman partner. I told him about the Hooray Henry giving me grief and that he was after a taxi to take him home, so my ex-doorman partner told me he would turn his car round and come back and pick up the Hooray Henry to save me. I turned off the phone call. I was about to tell the Hooray Henry there was a taxi coming to pick him up, but to be honest, I didn't want to talk to him and thought I would just wait until my ex-doorman partner turned up in his taxi to pick him up. Hooray Henry was staggering all over the place, and when he was standing still, he was swaying like a flower in a hurricane.

My ex-doorman partner pulled up in his taxi real slow outside the venue, and as he did, Hooray Henry fell back into the road onto the bonnet of the taxi! That's all it was, a fall back onto a taxi, and to be honest, if the taxi hadn't been there to break his fall, then Hooray Henry would have probably fallen a lot worse and cracked his head.

Now, for some crazy mysterious unexplained Arthur C Clarke reason, nobody saw Hooray Henry fall back on to the car; all they heard was the thud of his body hitting the bonnet of the car and then seeing him rolling about on the floor. The reason he was rolling about was because he was trying to stand up! This is the guy that couldn't stand up when he was standing up! So, before you knew it we had an over-reacting pissed-up tart screaming like she'd just witnessed a mass murder, a pissed-up bloke who watched 'Holby City' once a month and now thinks he's a doctor, a screaming wannabe famous nobody screaming, "I saw the whole thing, I saw the whole thing; nobody move!" As he brushed his hair with the back of his hand, dreaming of interviews and pictures with the local press. People starting to gather round throwing in their opinions and just all talking shit. I thought to myself, 'This is going to end badly for my ex-doorman partner'.

My ex-doorman partner jumped out of his taxi, gave me a wink, went over to Hooray Henry and, putting his arm under his armpit, started laughing and looked at the lynch mob, saying, "It's okay, folks. No need to worry; he does this all the time, it's his party trick! He's a stuntman. He always does this to me; you must know him? Seen him in a few films? Anyway, I gotta go - his missus has just rung me to get him home because he's filming tomorrow."

I was thinking to myself, 'No fucking way are these going to believe what he just said! If he blags this, next time I'm in Court, I'm hiring him for my Barrister'. So, what happened? They only start taking selfies with the Hooray Henry as he was getting put into the back of the taxi! My ex-doorman partner shut the back door of the taxi and jumped into the front, closed the door and drove off, throwing me a wink and a cheeky smile.

The next night on the door, the police turned up and started asking me questions about an incident the night before, when a member of the public had been mown down by a car and had received serious life-threatening injuries. Fuck sake! I was in a right pickle now. I had to do what was right but then there was the code of honour of not being a grass and so on and so forth. I had a million thoughts buzzing through my head. The police were still talking to me but nothing was registering with me. Over the shoulder of the police officer, I saw a taxi pull up on the roadside. I recognised the taxi; it was my ex-doorman partner. I was wondering how I could signal him to clear off. Then the back door opened and out stepped the 'Hooray Henry' from the night before! He was looking considerably more sober now, and he started walking towards me. I heard the laughter from the taxi of my ex-doorman partner. My head was frying now - what the fuck was going on here? It turned out when the police officer was talking to me and I switched off, he was on about a completely different incident to the one the night before outside the venue I was working.

My ex-doorman partner got out of his taxi and came running towards me. "I gotta be quick," he said, laughing. He gave a nod and a laugh to the police who hadn't finished dealing with me; they looked at him in bemusement and just let him carry on. He went on to tell me that while driving 'Hooray Henry' home, he struck up a conversation, told 'Hooray' that he'd stepped in front of his taxi and rolled over his bonnet like a stuntman, and that loads of women were having selfies with him thinking he was famous. He said, 'Hooray Henry' loved it and sobered up double-quick as he was telling him the story, that when he dropped him off at his big house, he paid his fare, gave him a tip, offered to pay for any damage he might have caused to his taxi and took his mobile number so he could use him as his personal taxi driver.

Talk about falling in a barrel of shit and coming out smelling of roses? I think my ex-doorman partner should be writing a book:

'One night in a taxi'.

40.

Rambo

One night on the door, I was working this venue, an alright place. I'd worked better and worked worse. To tell you the truth, I had worked a lot better and a lot worse! For some reason, I stuck it out working there, probably because they paid us very well. This one particular night, I got talking to a nice young lady, whom, for reasons of National Security we shall call Jane, and she told me she was from a distance away and just moved into the area with her parents. She said that she had travelled the world because her father was in the forces. She went on to tell me about her father being a PTI in the forces, about how hard her father was in the forces, about how her father was of some high-class rank in the forces. I started thinking to myself that she must be the daughter of John Rambo! I was waiting for the stories of how he stormed the enemy nest and, single-handed, captured a platoon of soldiers. So, I was doing my best to look interested and every now and then saying, "Really? Did he really? Wow, he's some man," and in my mind, I had this vision of her dad looking like a Chippendale with the body of John Rambo but bigger and harder.

Jane cleared off into the venue to be with her friends, and I carried on doing my doorman bit for the night. Every now and then, Jane walked past and smiled; you know the kind of smile I'm talking about, the one that would get you a part in a toothpaste advert. At the end of the night, my Jane was back talking to me, asking me if I would like to give her a lift home. Now, I'm not one to see a damsel in distress so I kindly agreed to give her a lift home.

On the way driving from the venue to her house, Jane told me that she lived with her mum and dad and that we would have to be quiet when we got to her house. I was gutted now. I thought she had her own place and lived on her own. I mean, how the fuck am I going to be quiet if John Rambo is at home? He can hear an ant fart from 200 metres away! But, I thought, 'Fuck it, I'm only giving her a lift home'.

We arrived at her house and she asked me the line of all lines -

"Would you like to come in for a coffee?" I wish I had a pound for every time I've heard that said. Sometimes, when that was said, I wanted to reply, "It's a bit late for coffee; have you got any Horlicks in?" but then again, I thought it might spoil the moment.

I decided to risk it and agreed to go into the house for a coffee. Part of me was loving the fact of living dangerously, and part of me was nervous I might get tied up by grass and thrown into a bamboo cane prison they might keep under the stairs. We entered the house through the back door which led us into the kitchen; so far so good; no tripwires, holes in the ground covered up by camouflage lino, and no guard dogs. Jane walked over to the kettle and flicked on a switch. The kettle started to make a slight rumbling noise as it heated up. Jane walked towards me and I knew where this was going. How, you ask me? Because it's always the same; the kettle gets flicked on, but the cups never ever get put out. That's what always happens in these 'do you fancy a coffee' situations.

Just as we were about to tongue-wrestle, there came a noise from upstairs. Now I'd gone from half-living dangerously and half-nervous to full-on nervous! I knew it was going to be Rambo with his black SAS pyjamas and black balaclava on, getting out of bed to sharpen his knife before he reached for his flame thrower!

"Look, maybe I should get off and see you another time," I said to Jane with a dry mouth. "You know, it's getting late and I've got to be at Sunday School early tomorrow morning."

Jane just laughed at me and told me everything was okay, that her dad wouldn't come down the stairs, he'd probably be just going to the toilet. I was thinking, 'He won't come down the stairs because he's going to abseil down the side of the house and come crashing through the kitchen window'. My head was a mess; I'd heard all Jane's stories all night about her father. I could tell that they were close and I knew that he was going to torture anybody who went near his daughter unless they had good intentions. I needed to get out, but it was too late now. I heard the creak of what I knew was a top hallway stair; all top hallway stairs creak the same, no matter if it's a new house or an old house; even in bungalows they creak the same (think about it)!

I heard another thud and then another! Rambo was coming down the stairs! My palms were getting sweaty. I was trying to remember all my karate moves and wondering if they would work if I did them double-quick. The thud on the stairs stopped - I knew now he was seconds away from opening the door- I saw the kitchen door handle start to turn. I was scared (don't tell anybody) and my adrenaline was rushing on full flow. My mind was in fight or flight mode when the door opened and there he stood in front of me.

Now, I wanted to say, "Who the fuck are you?" but first impressions and all that malarkey. I was looking at what stood in front of me and then turned and looked at Jane, waiting for her to explain why her smaller older brother was out of bed. Nope, did she fuck; she did her toothpaste smile, swayed her arm towards the man in front of me and said, "Martin, I'd like you to meet my dad."

Now you've got to understand; I was nervous. I had adrenaline rushing through my body, my mind was already set at fight or flight mode, and to top it off, Jane had got my name wrong...

WHO THE FUCK WAS MARTIN?!!!!!!!!!!!!!

You've got to understand - I had all that pent up inside me and stood in front of me was a little fat Jimmy Krankie lookalike with a comb-over haircut, wearing stripy pyjamas! I mean, I don't underestimate people by the way they look; learnt that myself at a young age in karate tournaments, getting my arse kicked for underestimating my opponents, but this man who was in front of me, who, all night, I had been hearing all these glorious war stories about and supposedly had the body of Adonis and was super strong, was shaped like an egg and about the size of an egg! That'll be a chicken egg, not an ostrich egg, because an ostrich egg is bigger than him. I couldn't contain my emotions and they got the better of me,

"What were you, a PTI instructor in the fucking boy scouts? You fucking little midget dumpy short-legged gimp, your whole body is about as big as Rambo's big toenail, you couldn't fight your way out of a wet paper bag and I bet the only medals you have got are for 50-metre breaststroke. Jeezzzzuuussss, you have had me on edge all night and look at you!"

As I started to head for the door to get out of there, I saw a movement out of the side of my eye. I instantly knew it was a dog but didn't have the time to register what kind of dog before it was on my ankle, growling and snarling and tearing the bottom of my trousers to shreds.

The father was screaming at me, " Get out, get out of my house, you fucking animal, you're a disgrace!"

Meanwhile, Jane was shouting at me, "Get him, Rambo, get him; kill, Rambo, kill!" Now, I was halfway out of the door with my leg still being pulled back into the kitchen by the dog, which I knew then was a Jack Russell called Rambo, unless it was Jane shouting at her dad to get me and kill me. The dog eventually released its grip, I think because it was knackered from redesigning the bottom of my trousers, the little mutt.

Just as I got to my car, Jane came walking up behind me.

"You messed with the wrong family; you're a marked man," she said in a bit more of a calm state now.

As I got into my car, I turned round and looked at her. I couldn't help myself - I had to do it, and I said to Jane, "Don't push me!"

41.

Protein Farts

One night on the door, I was working this venue, a nice place; always busy. It had been a bit naughty when we first started working there, but we got it sorted out. There was no more trouble and it turned into a right easy number to work. This venue was split into two parts; one side was a nice restaurant which served quality food and had a very good reputation for serving food, and the other side of the venue was a bar that was always busy. In between was the foyer where we used to stand working the venue, where we could keep an eye on the front door and see who was entering the premises. We could see the patio area to one side and the smoke shelter to the other side, then every couple of minutes or so we would walk around the outside of the venue and the car park to check everything was okay, then have a walk into the bar and check the toilets for any punters who might have been having nasal problems. It was very rarely we made our presence felt in the restaurant; there was no need to. I mean it was not as though we were going to be involved in food fights or somebody was going to get assaulted with a sausage! Well, they might get assaulted later with a sausage but that's a different story.

There was only three of us worked this venue, and I had a pool of six lads to choose from. The lads in the pool, apart from one, were all bodybuilding fanatics, always eating correctly, one week dieting, the other week taking on loads of sugar, no carbs another week. To be honest, it did my nut. They had mood swings; one week they were happier than a fat kid in a cake shop and the next week they were angrier than a fat kid in a health spa. One of the good things about working this venue was that at the beginning of our shift, we used to get offered free food if we wanted it, like a tuna sandwich or chicken sandwich, a plate of chips and whatever else was healthy; nothing to heavy, just a snack. Of course, working with the bodybuilders, they never refused food of any kind.

One night, we were stood in the foyer chatting away when one of the waitresses from the bar came to see us and asked us if we wanted some tuna sandwiches and chips. We kindly accepted the offer. I also asked her for a cup of tea to go with my sandwich, but the other two lads working with me declined the cup of tea, saying they had some protein shakes in the car and would rather drink one of them because they were bulking up. I thought to myself, 'They already look bulked up, pair of fat cunts'. So, the food came and I ate my sandwiches and I drank my cup of tea. They had their sandwiches and drank their protein shakes from some kind of ugly plastic container.

The night progressed and we did our routines of checking different areas of the venue. At one point in the night, I did the car park and surrounding area of the venue, and as I walked back into the venue, I was smashed in the face by an absolutely horrendous awful stench! It was so vile I started to nearly vomit. I start thinking to myself, "What the fuck is going on? We're under a terrorist attack with stink bombs!' I grabbed hold of one of the front doors that led from the outside to the foyer and I started swinging the door quickly to cause a draught to try and get rid of the smell. While I was doing this, two couples left the restaurant and walked into the foyer and straight into the wall of stench. All four of them immediately pulled contorted faces, started to rush towards the doorway where I was standing swinging the door, but as they made their mad dash for life-saving fresh oxygen, the door I was swinging hit one of the men in the face. He swung round, grabbing his face, and in the same motion, his elbow struck one of the women in the face! She screamed out and covered her face with her hands, but I already knew she had damage to her nose before I saw the sight of her blood!

"You fucking prick, what the fuck do you think you're doing?" shouted the man who had been door-damaged.

"Sorry, mate, I was trying to get rid of the smell," I said back to the injured man in a sympathetic tone. I was already thinking to myself that this was going to turn out bad; I don't know how but I just knew it was. Then, the doors from the bar opened and out walked a couple of young lads with beers in their hands, which normally meant that they would be heading for the smoke shelter for a cigarette. They took two steps into the foyer and were hit by the smell; it was the face they pulled that give it away,

"What the fuck is that smell?" shouted one of the lads, looking at his mate. His mate screwed up his face and just started to laugh. They both hurried past the injured man and woman stood in the doorway, looked them up and down and then one of the young lads said to the injured woman, "Have you done that? It fucking stinks," and started laughing and so did his mate, upon which the other man who was with the couples threw a punch at the young lad who asked the question. His punch was nothing special; obviously the man had no training in any kind of boxing or martial arts. As quick as the man had thrown the punch, the young lad's friend reacted by throwing a punch back, and all this while the stench of 1000 drains was still lingering and my two doormen were nowhere to be seen.

Now, I had to let go the door I was wafting to try and get rid of the smell. I placed my body between the young lads and the men, positioning myself at an angle so I could scope the situation and that my back and front were not facing either of the warring parties. Still no sign of my doormen! What seemed to have been going on for a long time actually happened in the course of less than two minutes. I heard a bang of the bar-room door being opened frantically behind me and the rush of numerous bodies, and the high-pitched moaning of women and the low tones of men moaning, and even though they were all moaning at once and probably all saying different things, all I heard was, "What the fuck is that smell?" The herd of punters came galloping towards the door where I was stood. I managed to shimmy out the way like a gazelle; not so lucky for the warring parties though. The young lads and the two couples got swept away in the herd of punters, and still no show of my doorman partners. Surely, they would turn up now, with all this going on, wondering where I was, if I was okay. That's not a doorman thing; that's just human nature, but they were still nowhere to be seen. Now, I was stood outside amongst a crowd of people all coming down with the deadliest symptoms of poison I have ever seen. Some of them were looking towards me to save them, save their lives. Now they were looking at me not as a doorman but as some kind of superhero who could save their lives. Fuck that! I was pissed off. They would have to call some other caped crusader! I was off to find the fucking two numpty doormen who had gone missing in my time of need.

I started to walk back through the foyer and into the bar. I was confronted by the bar manageress, with a scrunched-up face. Straight away, she started screaming that the doormen were animals, that they stink and that they made her feel sick! I hadn't got a clue what she was on about and by now I was past caring because my night had just gone crazy, but in the life of a doorman, you always expect the unexpected. What most people think of as crazy, working the doors, it is just the norm.

Beside the bar was the men's toilet, and as I approached the toilet there was a smell; sorry, there was an unbearable stench coming from that direction. I didn't want to walk any further towards the toilet; the area was clear of punters, so I shouted out, "Oi! What the fuck is going on?" just knowing the doormen who watched my back were in there. Seconds later, one of my doormen appeared with fingers squeezing the nose on his face and a stupid grin on his face. He looked at me and opened his mouth to tell me something but no words came out; he just bent over and started laughing.

"What the fuck are you laughing about? I ain't laughing; I'm fucking pissed off!" and I was fucking pissed off at how the night was turning out and how unprofessional we were looking. The doorman eventually gained composure and lifted his head and said to me, "He has shit himself; he went to do a protein fart and followed through, that is why there is the awful smell!"

I couldn't believe it, and as much as I wanted to block it out, all that was running through my mind was the amount of gunk that would have come out of that carpet-carrying elephant arse of his and be running down his leg. But I had to save the day and save the venue's reputation,

So, I said, "Right get your arse back in there and get him and take him out the fire exit at the back of the venue. Avoid the punters, and get him to fuck in his car. Once he has gone, you come back and we'll finish the shift together."

I headed back to the foyer and through the door to where all the customers were. I looked at them, stood there all confident and shouted out, "It's okay, folks, we've fixed the problems with the drains. Get yourselves back in there; there are free shots for everybody!"

A big cheer was given and the punters all stampeded back to the bar. Do I think they believed the drain story? Do I fuck.

Do I think the bar manageress was going to believe the drain story? Do I fuck.

But most importantly, do I think the owner of the venue would believe the drain story? Do I fuck.

So, what happened next was I had to explain to the owner of the venue what happened. I paid the bar bill of shots for all the punters that night, which meant I worked for nothing, I gave shitty arse the sack and told him I hoped he stuck to wearing nappies instead of boxer shorts. From then on, doormen were banned from eating on the door at this venue and under strict orders to always have a bailout before coming to work.

UXF UXB

Unexploded fart

42.

Alfa Romeo

One night on the door, I was working this venue. It was in my early days of working the doors, a nice smart busy place. Nobody gave me a second look on the door; no woman gave me a second look and no man gave me a second look. My confidence in working the door was taking a dive, but I wasn't bothered as long as I got paid at the end of the night. I suppose I was like an apprentice, really. I worked with some of the old-school doormen who were big ugly old bully boys and they didn't really like me because of my youth and boyish looks. The reason I got the job was because my boxing coach knew the new manager there and put my name forward. The new manager was spot on with me; he was not much older than me and he hated the old-school bully doormen and wanted rid of them, so this night I got a new partner who turned out to be the new manager's school friend. He was okay and we hit it off straight away. He was a carpet carrier (bodybuilder) but he was all natural he told me, no steroids. He ordered a half-pint of Guinness while we were working on the door. I told him I didn't drink while working the door; at that time, I hardly drank at all (oh how times have changed). He told me he was looking after his mate's car for the weekend and that it was a top, top sports car, (for the protection of all concerned I can't reveal what car). I couldn't believe it; I told him he must have some really trusting mates, as the lads I grew up with would not trust me to look after their bike for the weekend, let alone their car, and definitely not a sports car. He carried on telling me how fast it was, brake horsepower, cylinders, pistons, tyre width, and loads of other mechanical petrol-head shit and I didn't have a clue what he was talking about. I was just nodding my head, looking interested, giving the occasional nod saying, "Oh really?" but all that was going through my head was, 'Are we taking it out for a spin after work and is he going to let me drive the top, top sports car'? Eventually, I plucked up the courage, to be honest, more out of boredom. I asked him if we were going to take the car for a spin after work. He looked a bit shocked that I had asked him. He took like what seemed an eternity to reply, then reluctantly said, "Okay then, we'll take it for a quick spin after working the door."

"Nice one," I replied.

That night on the door seemed to drag. Eventually, we got to closing time. We managed to get everybody out the venue pretty quick, quicker than normal; that might have been a bit to do with me. We left the venue and I headed with my new doorman friend to where my car was parked. He told me he was parked in the same car park as me. I had a Red Vauxhall Calibra at the time; I loved it; very fast and a good-looking car. My new friend went to get in the car parked beside mine which was a standard Ford Escort. I looked at the car thinking maybe it was a top, top-secret fast car, like one of those cars James Bond uses. I asked him if that was the top sports car he was on about, half in jest and half-serious. He told me it wasn't and that the top, top sports car was parked at his house.

"Okay, I'll come to yours then; where do you live?" He told me his address and we both set off to his house. I didn't really know the area he lived in, but when I arrived at his house, it was in a state. He was halfway through home improvement. There, on the drive, was this top, top sports car, and even though it was midnight, it was shining in the gleam of the moon. You could see it was power, it was class; the same colour as my Vauxhall Calibra, except now my very fast Vauxhall Calibra was starting to look like a homemade go-cart compared to this beast of a machine.

My friend asked me inside his house while he went to get the keys.

"What do you think?" he asked me with a smug grin on his face.

I didn't need to reply; the smile on my face said it all.

"Go in the kitchen, mate, and get some chicken out the oven. I'm just gonna nip upstairs and get changed," he shouted to me as he ran up the stairs.

I thought to myself, 'Why do all these bodybuilder-type doormen I work with eat chicken all the time?' That's all they do! Sometimes I would be working the doors with bodybuilders and they would turn up with packing-up boxes full of chicken; chicken nuggets, chicken breasts, chicken legs, chicken fucking popcorn. I used to wonder if ever they were on a night out and they started drinking spirits, if they ever would put chicken gravy granules in their drink as a mixer? It used to proper ruffle my feathers. Anyway, I wasn't a bodybuilder, but I did like to eat, well it would be rude not to, so I got myself some chicken out the oven, which was nice.

My friend came down the stairs and shouted, "You ready? "

I couldn't reply; I had a mouthful of chicken. I just grunted a sound that sounded like "Yeah".

We both got in the car and he started it up. It sounded like it looked, awesome! We drove off down the street, keeping within the speed limits; I think my friend was a bit wary of waking and annoying his neighbours, which I could understand. He looked at me; "Is this not the best car you've ever been in? We'll go to the motorway and I will really show you what it can do!"

"Let's do it," I replied, but all I was thinking was, 'I want to drive this top, top sports car'. We came up to our last roundabout heading out of town and onto the motorway. Soon, as we came out of the curve and were heading straight, he put his foot down on the accelerator. The force pinned me back against my seat! My friend started laughing - "The Eagle has landed" he said. To this day, it has always bugged me that he said that. We were doing well over the speed limit down the motorway and he was talking about a bird sitting on a perch! And why didn't he say 'the chicken has landed' and keep within the theme of me telling this story? 'WEIRDO'.

We travelled roughly 5 miles down the motorway, and came to the turnoff to head up and then go back on the opposite side of the motorway. He asked me if I would like to drive it back; that was like asking a bodybuilder if he liked chicken.

"I don't believe it, aww fuck, fuck, fuck, fuck!" my friend started saying, looking in the car's rear-view mirror.

And without even asking, I knew what he was going to say. I turned my head to look out of the window and somewhere back in the darkness of the night, I could see blue lights flashing,

"Quick, get back on the other side of the motorway and head back for town. If they come up the slip road and head back down the same way, they're probably after us."

We did that, and we were flying, and sure enough, in the view of the street lights behind us, we saw the car head up the slip road and then reappear on our side of the motorway. I told him just before we got back to town, at the first roundabout there was a turn off to an industrial estate with all kinds of slip roads and various different exits. I told my friend to head there. He was in a panic; the nerves had kicked in. You could tell he'd never really been a naughty boy; about his only dealings with the police was when he took his cycling proficiency badge.

We took the turning for the industrial estate and I told him to drive slowly through, not drawing the attention of security guards, and if the police used any CCTV, which wasn't very good back at that time, and it picked the top, top sports car,, he could sort an alibi out for when they visited.

We managed to get through the industrial estate without speeding or seeing any blue lights behind us. We were steadily getting through town, when my friend started to get a bit cocky, thinking we had got away from the police. That was not my way; police are a lot cleverer than people give them credit for.

"One last burst, eh, before we park up?"

I was about to reply, "Let's just get back to your house and park up," but I didn't get chance. He put his foot down on the accelerator and we were off! We were on a main road in town, a built-up area of old Victorian terraced houses, with cars parked on both sides of the road. Out in front of us, an old white Ford Cortina pulled across us from the other side of the

251

road with no lights on. My friend hit the brakes at the same time as beeping the car horn. we skidded, the Cortina tried to pull out of the way, but both cars crashed into one another side by side. Both cars came to a stop together. We got out and assessed the damage, then the White Ford Cortina sped off, well, drove off. I looked at my friend and said, "Quick! Get back in the car!" We both got back in as lights from the houses around us started to come on to see what the commotion was.

I told him, "Drive home quick; there's only one explanation for what just happened there - that driver of the Cortina was pissed, a drunk driver. You can't report him because you were speeding and the police from the motorway might be after you and if they attended here, you're fucked!"

He nodded his not so cocky head in agreement.

We arrived at his house and parked up. He was a bag of nerves again. I told him to calm down and asked him if I could have some more chicken out the oven. I began to tell him he was in the clear; the Police hadn't caught up with him from the motorway and the owner of the White Cortina would not say anything because they were pissed.

"Yeah, but what about all the damage to the car? How the fuck am I going to explain that to my friend?" he tearfully spat out.

"Just tell him the truth and pay for the damage! Can I have some more chicken? Then I'm going."

At this point of the night, I left him. The next night on the door, he never turned up. The new manager of the venue, who was his friend, told me he was never working the door again because he'd had the worst experience of his life.

After I left my chicken-eating carpet-carrying friend, he decided to try and be clever and take the car somewhere and burn it out, then his plan was to tell his friend, if the police rang him about speeding or crashing, that it had been pinched off his drive, so he burned the car out. Next morning, his friend rang him and said the police had been in touch about his car speeding down the motorway and being found burnt out, but burnt out with the keys still in the ignition. Luckily, the owner had a cast-iron alibi, which he would have because he never did it! He made some excuse that his car must have been stolen from his house and never dropped my now-to-be-ex-doorman friend in trouble. Only problem was, he left the car thinking the doorman would not be taking the top, top sports car out for a rally experience, so he had cancelled his insurance, so now he was telling the doorman he had to compensate him for not dropping him in it. I wouldn't like to speculate on the cost of replacing that car, but I heard the doorman had paid for it all with loads of overtime at work. I think he got some money from his house supposedly being burgled, and I heard he started breeding chickens and selling their eggs. I wouldn't have minded seeing his chicken run.

43.

Frank Savage V Lily Bruno

One night on the door, I was working this venue; a rave club. Everything was going on in there, sex, drugs, business deals, wheeling, dealing, squealing, peeling, that fucked-up feeling; the music they played was great. I used to struggle not to start dancing while working the door. I loved the place; the doormen were always getting the DJs to make them cassette recordings of the music being played, then we were always playing the music down at the boxing gym, and the like. I have most of it copied now to USB or CD (Yeah that's right; I'm down with the technology).

So, this one Saturday night, the place was in full swing, bouncing; good vibes, no trouble; you could sense there wasn't going to be any trouble - doormen have that sixth sense - sometimes they can be wrong about it, but it's very rare, and they always stay switched on regardless.

This particular night, I was partnered with a doorman who was having a bit of trouble at home with his missus. His mind wasn't on the job, his mind was somewhere else. He looked vacant; to be honest, he always looked like that because he was a couple of sandwiches short of a picnic, and a flask, and maybe some knives and forks. Basically, he was thick as pig shit and looked like pig shit. He thought Moby Dick was a sexual disease, bless him. I felt sorry for him that night, but then after the third time of him telling me the same story about his troubles at home, I realised probably why his partner wanted to leave him.

I had heard rumours they used to fight a lot, and sometimes he would show up to work with a black eye. Sometimes you would see her walking round town with a few bruises; we nicknamed her Panda Anderson because of her black eyes. I felt like topping myself listening to his stories that particular night.

I mean, I would understand where his feelings were coming from if his partner was a looker, but she was just as ugly as him. To be honest, she looked like him but with a wig on. To give you some kind of idea how they looked, remember in the film ET when he was dressed up for Halloween? Well, that was the look and body shape of his partner. I could see he was itching for trouble to start so he could release some pent-up aggression, so I was doing my best to talk him down and take the aggression out of him, installing a bit of the old 'WAD RYU' - you know, a bit of the old 'PEACE AND HARMONY' - tell him everything would be okay, that he and his partner were a match made in heaven (more like a match made in Star Trek). One minute he was nodding his head and agreeing with what I was saying, the next he was close to tears, shaking his head and repeating the same shit he'd been telling me all night. I started to hope myself that a fight would kick off and that I would get beaten up and taken off to hospital, but knowing my luck, he would end up in the hospital bed next to me! I'm not saying I have bad luck, but I'm the sort of guy that if, someday, my boat came in, I'd be stood at the fucking airport.

A call came through on my radio to go to the dancefloor, so both me and my partner were off, no hesitation. I'd got his back and he'd got mine. I knew that as we got there, the other doormen working with us would be there. We reached the dancefloor; nothing to be seen. Everybody was dancing, there was nothing out of place, the usual moves and shapes were being thrown. I quickly got on the radio to tell the other lads to stand down as it was a false alarm. I turned to give my partner the nod that we were good to go back to our station, and as I did so, I saw him talking to a man-mountain of muscle - well, I didn't really know if it was a man-mountain or a woman-mountain - he/she was dressed as a woman in a scantily-laced dress with no sleeves revealing huge muscly arms and the person had long blonde hair, which had to be a wig because he/she was black; it was like looking at Frank Bruno with long blonde hair. My doorman partner was stood up on his tiptoes shouting in his ear, then he would lean forward, drop his head and shout back in his ear. It was like a little made-up dance. I started making my way off the dancefloor towards my station, then I noticed out of the corner of my eye that my partner and Lilly Bruno were following me, still talking away. When I got back to my station, the other doormen were there. They looked at me, looked over my shoulder then looked back towards me and asked me what was going on.

"Fucked if I know," I replied, "I think he's pulled!"

They all started laughing. My partner never noticed us laughing and stood with his back to the wall just to the side of me. I could see he was pouring his heart out to Frank Savage, and Frank was nodding in agreement with whatever he was saying and consoling him with his great big hand resting on his shoulder.

After about 10 minutes of the two of them chatting together, they both walked towards me and my partner told me he was leaving; his mind was not on the job and that he was going to be giving his new mate a lift home because he was not feeling the vibe in there that night. At this, Frank Savage leant forward towards me and said,

"If I was you, I'd watch yourself in here tonight; it's full of weirdos - some very strange people!"

I was in shock! I was flicking through my brain asking myself if I had just heard that right, that he was calling people strange? I asked my mate if he was sure he wanted to get off. I was genuinely worried for him, but he told me everything was okay, and he seemed to be in a relaxed manner for the first time that night.

"Okay, mate, see ya later, you take care of yaself," I said, as they both headed for the door, "and don't do anything I wouldn't do".

God only knows what happened when they left that night, but he never worked the doors around our way again. He never got back with his partner; he moved away and the legend of the 'Brokeback Doorman' was started.

44.

Food Fight

One night on the door, I was working this venue; an alright place. Trade was steady and it was on the main drag of bars, pubs, clubs and restaurants. Just two of us worked this venue. It was not a very big place but had a steady turnover, but the turnover was never enough for the boss. The turnover was never, ever enough for any boss I worked for - they always wanted more - they were always looking to be the next Peter Stringfellow or J.D. Wetherspoon! So, the boss approached me and told me he was going to open the upstairs and see about booking it out, and try and get private functions on the go.

"Nice one; you know you'll need another doorman on to work, don't ya? Fire limits and crowd control and all that bollocks," I said to him. Already in my mind, I knew I was going to line the pocket of one of my friends (that's what it's all about).

"Yeah, I know, I know, that's why I have come to let you know; get a doorman sorted for next weekend," he replied, shaking his head with a leary grin; he knew I would push for that.

So, the following weekend, there were now three of us working the venue, two on the door and one floating about between the upstairs and down. We kept a rotation going of who would stand the door and who would float, but after a time, the rotation was being used; when or if it was more likely that somebody had a chance of giving somebody a lift home from upstairs, then they got the majority of the time to work upstairs, so the floating fell flat.

The upstairs private bookings surprisingly took off. I think the boss played it right; he gave the venue out for free, was happy with his alcohol takings, and he would let whoever was hiring the venue bring their food. All they had to do was pay for the DJ. At the end of the night, there was always food leftover from the parties; very rarely would the party people box it up and take it home. We always got offered food at the end of the night and always gladly accepted; be rude not to.

I think I might have said before that I've always worked in my life, from the age of 12, paper round, milk round, barrow boy on the docks, worked with my uncle who was a builder and these jobs were before I left school. Well, it was the same back then; I had a daytime job as well as working the door. At that time, I was working locally round the area, rigging. That particular time I was on a local oil refinery, so on a Saturday night, if there was a lot of food left over, I would box it up, put it in the boot of my car and take it to work the next morning. Depending on who I gave a lift home depended on what state the food ended up in the next day; if the car was rocking then the boxes or plates ended up becoming a mush of food. Sometimes my boot looked horrendous in the morning when I opened it up, but the lads at work loved it; I could keep our cabins going sometimes for days with quiche sarnies and all that. Made me popular; unless it was one of those times when they boxed up the food at the end of the night, then the next day I never took any food into work and you could guarantee that some bloke had forgotten his pack-up and I would be the biggest cunt walking. Feed all of the cabin some of the time, feed some of the cabin some of the time and feed none of the cabin some of the time, and I'd still be a cunt; bet that Barnum geezer never got any of that shit.

This one night on the door, we had a party going on upstairs, a mixed crowd of people, ages, styles. It was nice; no bad vibes in the air, everything going lovely. You could tell there was going to be no violence with this party, and as usual, I called it fucking wrong again! At the end of the night, the downstairs, opened to the public, was empty. We were just waiting for the party people to leave. I'd clocked the leftover food and I was fucking drooling at the mouth, and I was imagining driving home ramming the quiche into my mouth, beef and mustard sarnies dropping all over my car and how popular I was going to be the next morning at work.

All of a sudden, a woman screamed, one of those pissed-up aggro ladette screams. I turned to see a young lady (haha) with her hand in a fella's face. I had seen it a million times before and knew it was a lady having a row with her partner about him looking at another woman; without even knowing, I knew just by looking at the body language of them both. But I didn't know that the lady's (haha!) sister was the cause of the argument and would throw a sandwich at the arguing couple, at which the lady (haha!) would then storm over to the buffet table, pick up an open egg and cress sandwich and throw it back at her and miss, hit some fella who then turned and laughed, and shouted those fucking dreaded words I never wanted to hear at any party:

"FOOD FIGHT!!!!!!!!!!!!!"

Before myself or my door staff could act, it was on. The air was a mass of food flying about! We steamed into the fray shouting at people to stop, trying to stand in front of the buffet table to stop these animals from wrecking my chance of moving up the popularity stakes the next morning at work. I mean, you read most doorman stories and they've been bitten, glassed, stabbed and shot, I had, apart from shot, but now I was being pork-pied, Pringled, sandwiched and vol-au-vented, and the worse was, the cheese, sausage and pineapple on a stick were fucking lethal - they'd take your eye out! Ninjas should use them instead of shuriken stars! At one point, I thought I could feel blood running down the side of my face then I realised it was coleslaw! I'd had enough; it was like a food version of Rourke's Drift. We were fighting a losing battle so I just turned round and lifted the table of food on its side and tipped it over. None of these party-goers were going to get on their hands and knees and pick up food to throw at each other, and sure enough, they didn't; they turned their attention to me, saying I was out of order and that I should pay for the food! A few of the men left at the party started puffing their chests out and acting hard; suited me; I wanted fisticuffs now. I was fucking lathered in food, the venue is lathered in food and in the background, the lady (ha fucking ha) and her partner were kissing and caressing in the most beautiful display of affection I had ever seen. All that was missing was the bluebirds above their tomato salsa-dripping heads. I wanted to ram a big pointed Dorito right into their tomato salsa!

After a load of finger-pointing threats, arguing and the usual gangster shit, threats of coming back to shoot me, I thought to myself, 'They'll probably come back and shoot me with a salad cream bottle or worse, beetroot my white shirt'. We managed to clear them off. I didn't hang about the venue like I normally did; I was pissed off, felt like I'd been working the door at a Harvest Festival that had been terrorist-attacked by a suicide bomber! I collected our wages, dished them out to the door staff and headed out the door. I felt sorry for the cleaners having to clean up that mess.

As I was walking through the crowds making my way to my car, I was getting funny looks, snide remarks, people laughing, people giggling, which was making me even angrier. I got to my car, opened my boot, took off my jacket, gave it a shake and put it inside the boot. I took off my shirt, wiped it around my head and neck, gave it a shake and placed that on top of my jacket. I looked round - nobody about - I took off my shoes, had another quick check around me and then took off my trousers, shook them and placed them on top of my shirt and jacket, put my shoes back on, shut the boot and got into my car. I drove home wearing a pair of shoes, my socks and my boxers; not a nice sight. As I was driving home wondering what the fuck had just happened, the blue lights appeared in my rear-view mirror. I shook my head as I pulled my car over to the side of the road, thinking to myself, "Can this night get any worse'?

The police cunt stable walked up to my car. My window was already down, ready to engage in conversation. He knew me; he looked through the window and saw how I was dressed, (or not dressed).

"What you been up to tonight, Matthew?" he said in his best Dixon of Dock Green voice. "Have we been naughty tonight, fighting, and got covered in blood, Matthew, or have we been caught on the job and had to do a runner out the back door, Matthew?"

I was really not in the mood. I told him I had been in a food fight while working the door and that my clothes were in the boot. He started laughing and gestured his partner over with his hand.

"Listen to this one," he said to his partner, laughing. "Tell me again, Matthew why you are on the verge of getting arrested for indecent exposure."

"Fuck off, you're boring. My clothes are in my boot; go check the CCTV at the venue. You ain't arresting me for indecent exposure; I'm sat in my car! I could be going swimming or I might be going to a party booked as a flabbergram! Behave yourself and go catch some proper criminals!" I told him.

"Right, that's it! Let's have you out the car, Matthew, I can smell drugs," the police cunt stable said back to me.

"I don't do drugs. I always get tested at work for drugs. You can probably smell a fart, but not drugs," I told him. He knew that I didn't do drugs.

"I know, I'm only kidding with you, Matthew, but with a story like that, you should be on drugs! Get yourself off home," he laughed at me.

"Thank you." And I genuinely meant those words, 'Thank you'.

I got home late, so I decided to sleep on the couch. That was the norm in my house after I came home late from the door. She didn't want me to wake her, and I was paranoid about her smelling perfume on me or smelling something else, besides, I never wanted to wake the wife. Fuck me, I'd rather wake Frankenstein in a Halloween mask than wake the wife.

A few hours later, I was up and off to work. With no pack-up, I stopped off at the garage, grabbed a Sunday morning paper, a pot noodle and some crisps. For some reason, I didn't fancy a sandwich that morning; think I was developing a phobia. I got to work, entered the cabin and the lads asked me where the trays and boxes of food were? So, I told them what had happened. They all started laughing, accusing me of making it up and eating all the buffet myself. I wasn't in the mood for them. I went into the changing room and started to put on my overalls and safety helmet, then my safety glasses. As I put on my safety glasses, a piece of carrot fell from behind my ear. It must have been lodged there from the coleslaw! As it dropped to the floor, some of my workmates saw it and began to laugh, then called the other lads into the changing room.

I was embarrassed and went as red as a tomato, egg on my face, I'm normally cool as a cucumber, the chips were down, I'm the big cheese on the job, you know, full of beans.

Well, that was me done, no more free buffet for the lads at work and no more was I the toast of the cabin.

45.

Wig Came Off

One night on the door, I was working this venue; rough as fuck. The doorman was rough as fuck, the alcohol was rough as fuck, the décor was rough as fuck, the music was rough as fuck, the rats stayed away from this place because it was rough as fuck, and guess what? The punters, they were rough as fuck! We were always fighting in this place, ALWAYS. We used to have a sweepstake at the beginning of the night on how many fights we would be having on the night. If you got the ticket with three fights or less, you know you were on a loser. Whenever the fighting kicked off in this place it was 90% of the time around or on the dancefloor. The DJ would turn off the music and call the doormen over the speakers to attend. Sometimes it was a good thing and sometimes a bad thing having the music turned off.

The mad thing about this venue was, they never barred anybody! The head doorman and a few of the other doormen used to drink in this venue all week and only work the door on a Friday and Saturday night, so anybody involved in any trouble in there was always going to be their friends. I think most times on a Sunday afternoon, they would be drinking and laughing about the escapades from the nights previous with the punters who had been involved in the fighting. This was always going to make the job harder for me and the other doormen, being outsiders to the venue. It never really bothered me as long as the doormen had my back while I was working, and they paid really good money to work this place, which was right, because we earned every penny. Even the pennies were rough as fuck.

This one night, we were on our fourth brawl of the night. I blamed the DJ who was rough as fuck. All the doormen were full-on dealing with this particular brawl. There were the usual women, rough as fuck, screaming, the rough as fuck noise of glasses being smashed, rough as fuck men shouting and joining in throwing punches. It was rough as fuck chaos; couldn't see how it was going to end. And as these thoughts entered my head, I had an out-of-body experience. All around me, everything just seemed to slow down and everybody seemed to turn and focus on the stage. I say stage; it was more of a hop-up box beside the DJ box. On the stage was one of the doormen, who looked to me to be doing a Native American rain dance. He was tapping his hand over his mouth, lifting his leg up, bending his body down towards his leg while hopping, and in his other hand, which he kept waving about, he had a big clump of hair. He was dancing like a sign of victory you used to see in these old John Wayne movies when the Comanches had scalped somebody! All the time, he had the biggest, daftest grin on his face. Eventually, the punters in the venue began to laugh; you could feel the tension ease. Fists were being lowered, hands that were strangling necks were being lowered, tight grips on clothing being released - it was a biblical moment, like Moses parting the waves, then a punter started to join in with making the Comanche noises, then another then another, and soon the whole venue was making Indian noises. I thought it was going to start raining on the dancefloor! I shook my head and started to laugh. The punter I had hold of started laughing along with me, then started making Comanche noises. I looked to see where my fellow doormen were. I eventually saw them, one by one, laughing at some bloke with a bald head and a red face; a red face through anger not a red face because of his genetics. Somebody, during all the fighting, had pinched his wig! I'm not saying it was a good wig on his head; I used to think it looked rough as fuck.

We eventually got everything settled down after the fighting. We were laughing about the carry on; people were passing us on the stairs, going to the toilets or leaving the venue, and they were all giggling and making Red Indian noises. Bald Eagle had asked us to stop and search everybody to find his wig, but we tried to explain, how could we? What if somebody had put it on their underwear, and we thought we'd found it, started to pull on the hair only to find it was bushy pubes? That was hard trying to explain that without laughing in his face. A while later that night, after a couple more fights, rumour come back to us that somebody had put a contract out for his wig to be stolen, then the counter-rumour was that Mr Bald Eagle had put out a contract on whoever had put out a contract on his wig contract. We never did find his wig that night. The following night, somebody put a dead rat by the DJ box with a piece of cardboard attached to it and Bald Eagle's name. So, another contract was put out! I don't know what all these contracts were about, what the terms and agreements were; knowing that venue, probably just a free pint. I found it quite hair-raising that contracts were being put out over wigs! I used to see the guy out and about quite regularly after that weekend, and you would always hear people making Native American Indian noises as he was walking about. He never ever saw the funny side. I always thought he was going to pull out a tomahawk on somebody sometime. As long as it wasn't me, I would have no need to call for the cavalry.

46.

Stag Do

MONKEYS APES CHIMPS BANANAS FIGHTING POLICE LINE UP

One night on the door, I was working this venue; a great place to work - great door staff, great bar staff, great glass collectors, great DJ. The gaffer of this great venue was okay; I'm not going to say great for reasons that occurred later on in my time working there. It was in a great location around lots of other great bars, great nightclubs and great kebab houses. We had great punters coming in night after night, great weekend visitors of great hen parties, great stag dos, great rugby clubs all in great fancy dress outfits. As you have probably worked out, it was GREAT.

This one night on the door it was summertime. We were full to the rafters with punters. We had a group of rugby players in; they were from another town over for the weekend playing one of our local clubs. They were dressed as primates, I say primates because they were more than just monkeys, they were gorillas, baboons, apes, chimps and orangutans, anything hairy that ate a banana was with this rugby club. I couldn't see my ex-wife with them, though. They looked fantastic! Some were wearing all-in-one primate outfits, some half-dressed as a primate, the rest of their body done in makeup and some primates were wearing masks; it was a mixed array of fancy dress and looked GREAT. Like any other rugby club, they were fun, having a GREAT time, which is lucky for us door staff, especially when there were only six of you and these rugby club nights out normally knocked about in double figures. To be fair, I've never had any bother with any rugby club in any venue I've ever worked; had some issues to deal with, but no trouble.

Me and my partner were working the front door taking in the great summer night and great atmosphere of the people milling about, when up to our door approached a stag do from out of town, also dressed as primates. Yep, the same outfits as the rugby club - monkeys, gorillas, baboons, apes, chimps and orangutans, same sort of mixture as the primates before them. I looked at my partner and said, laughing,

"Well, we can't turn them away, we'll be arrested for being primatist; I mean, let's get it right, all monkeys' lives matter,"

My partner cracked up in hysterics and nodded, agreeing with me, so we let them in, and told them to be on their best behaviour; no monkey business.

All was going well - it was a great night. I was admiring the sights walking up and down the street, when to my side, I heard the words from my door partner, 'I don't believe it; aww, this is just great!' I turned my head and then saw what he was referring to; another group of monkeys! I started thinking to myself, 'This isn't normal, it's got to be a wind-up. The world has gone bananas!' They approached the door to come in. I looked at my partner, then he returned the look and I already knew what he was thinking; we can't knock them back for being dressed as monkeys, gorillas, baboons, apes, chimps and orangutans, it's not right; it's primatist and all monkeys' lives matter.

So now, we were working the door, and our venue was looking like a scene out of the movie 'Planet of The Apes'. Now, I can't see into the future but I had a feeling this was not going to end up a great night. I was on edge; my spider sense was tingling, and then, to save the day, up turns a hen party; no, not dressed as monkeys, but dressed as policewomen. For some reason, the most popular outfit with hen parties is GI Janes or policewomen. They approached the door all rowdy, rowdy in a nice way, flirty, giggling, boisterous, cheeky, suggestive, touchy-feely; to be honest, I thought no different to the real WPCs I've had to deal with in my time on the door! The real WPCs were always touchy-feely, especially when putting on the handcuffs. So, we let the hen party into the venue; daren't not, to be honest - any doorman will tell you, never mess with a hen party, NEVER. The venue was proper bouncing now.

Now, as I already have told you at the beginning of the book, I don't want to talk about fighting. Fighting is boring; always the same, two different stories and then the truth when it comes to fighting, but let's just say it all kicked off in the venue. It was chaos! Just about everybody who was in there got arrested, which was weird seeing police rumbling with other police, man-handling (I mean person-handling, let's keep it PC, or should I say WPC) police then handcuffing them and throwing them into the back of a van, and as usual, us doormen were given no professional courtesy by the local constabulary. A quick word before they left of what had gone on and then ordered to turn up the next day at the police station. So, let me just take you straight to the police interviews, which for legal reasons, I cannot publish, so I'll give you a bit of an idea how the interview went.

PC Harkness: "So, you see the gorillas jump on the chimpanzees, is that correct?"

Me: "I'm not sure, but I think it looked like the gorillas were bullying the chimpanzees."

PC Harkness: "What do you mean you are not sure?"

Me: "Well, I couldn't really tell if it was gorillas; it might have been a baboon, but I didn't get to see the arse of the primates who jumped the chimpanzees. If they would have had a big red arse, I'd say they were baboons, judging by what I've seen on nature programmes, but I need to be sure; can we not do a line-up?"

PC Harkness looked at me menacingly, like I'm in his bad books

"No, I don't think we can do a line-up, do you?"

Me: "But surely we don't want to convict the wrong primate, do we? I'm sorry, it's not going swingingly, is it? But I'm doing my best," I replied, with a cheeky smile at my old friend. I think to myself, 'I'll put myself right in his bad books; I'll make a monkey out of him'.

PC Harkness: "Did you witness any other assaults? Anything that could help us with our enquiries?"

I sucked in a deep breath and got ready for my masterpiece of a wind-up. "Look, I really want to help you in your investigation with all the alleged assaults, injuries, criminal damage and vandalism, but the whole night just went from being great to bananas. The first lot of primates came walking down the street and was getting the funniest looks from everyone they met, they weren't looking for trouble, they were just singing and monkeying around, hey, hey, they were just monkeys. Then the second lot of primates came along and were the same really. I mean, I don't want to say all primates look the same in case I offend, but they do! The trouble started really when the hen party of WPCs turned up. The atmosphere changed a little; it just seemed to go bananas, then when you guys turned up, (the real police) well, it all got very confusing. I mean you were making Tarzan noises; one monkey getting beat with a plastic or rubber truncheon looks the same as getting beat with a real truncheon, and to see police (the real police) arresting other police was all very confusing for me, so, PC Harkness, I would really want to help you as much as I can, but unless you do some kind of line-up of primates and police, I'm not very much help. You all look the same to me; surely the CCTV can help in convicting these animals. I really don't want to waste your time or the time of the Courts by having to stand in the witness box and swear under oath that a gorilla harmed a chimpanzee when it might have been a baboon, or even an orangutan. Or that I saw police assaulting other police and shouting at them, "Stop resisting, stop resisting"; the police always shout that when making arrests as it looks good for them in court if the accused is battered and bruised. The witnesses will say they saw the accused resisting arrest, but they never saw it, they just heard the police shouting "stop resisting arrest".

PC Harkness rubbed his head in his hands, looked at his colleague and decided to end the interview. He went on to tell me that he could arrest me for wasting police time. 'Good luck with that charge', I thought to myself, 'you must be nuts'.

"All I have done is tell the truth about what I saw," I said.

PC Harkness then told me I would probably receive a summons through the post to attend Court as a witness, and once again I think to myself, 'Good luck with that, you definitely are nuts.'

After all the carry on, the monkeying about, the police interviews, endless pointless letters over the months, nothing ever came of that night. No primates were charged, no WPCs were charged and no doormen were charged, WHICH WAS GREAT.

47.

Double Trouble

One night on the door, I was working this one-off rave. The organiser was a good friend of mine; I had known him since he was a young lad starting out. He was a cheeky fucker; didn't give a fuck and he was into all sorts of mischief. I liked him, so he asked me to supply some doormen, and he'd supply the rest, his own lads, but he needed registered doormen for the council to get the go-ahead. Registered doormen at that time usually had no or very little criminal record, but nowadays, a registered doorman has to have no record. He paid well so I had no problem recruiting six good lads, all registered and above board, for the books for the council. We kept two registered doormen and an unregistered doorman on the door and kept a rotation going that night. I knew all of the other non-registered doormen through one way or another; no problems - all good lads. The night was going okay, the usual rave carry on, loads of dancing, sweaty bodies, gurning, seen it all before. One of my registered doormen came up to me and told me there was a bit of trouble going on by the front door, so I rushed to the door and saw two unregistered doormen arguing with one of my registered doormen. I don't know what had gone on; first impressions to me was it was the Alpha male ego kicking in. It was not like we were all working together for me, even though we were all working together for me. And here was my situation; I had to try and calm down a 6ft 2inch hard man ex-convict who didn't care and had a police record for many crimes, his friend, another 6ft 2inch lunatic ex-convict who was one of the most violent men I had ever met, arguing with one of my registered doormen who was a 6ft 1inch ex-para, but didn't like the civilian way of life so was doing his SAS territorial training to go back to that way of life. Talk about a rough day at work! In my mind, I knew who was going to win this if they kicked off with each other, but then I also knew the two losers wouldn't let it stop at that; without a doubt, there would be repercussions, and then there would be repercussions on top of the repercussions! I stepped up to try and calm the situation down, but I had no chance - I was pissing in the wind. Nobody was listening to my reasoning or my charm, gutted really, I always thought I was quite charming (yeah right). What was seconds seemed like hours. I was thinking, 'If anybody throws the first punch here, I've got no chance of trying to stop it'. Not that I was going step in between them to break it up anyway - a loose haymaker off any of them would knock me out or break my jaw, and I didn't know if the lunatic would be carrying a knife; that was his forte on the street.

I had to think fast; it was going to take some kind of brains over brawn, some kind of kidology, psychology, or just some kind of blatant lie. At the door approached what seemed like a rugby club. I don't know why they appeared; you don't normally see beer monsters at a rave, big hulking leery-looking fuckers, so I just shouted out to my three arguing non-registered and registered doormen,

"Here's that other doorman agency supposed to be sorting you lot out and taking over the door tonight. They said you lot

276

are fuck all; they're going to take the money out of your pockets, and run what's going on in there."

The arguing stopped, the three of them looked at the hulking figures, who you could see had no reason to be there as they weren't coming to dance, more likely kick off. The tension switched to three onto six, seven, maybe 8. I just turned and walked away back up the stairs into the club, the noise of music in front of me, the noise of fighting behind me, big noise fighting. I thought to myself, 'I'll give it five or ten minutes, then go back and see how they are'. I bumped into the organiser of the event, and he asked me if everything was okay, was I having a good time? He was glad there was no trouble. I thought to myself, 'Why do I let myself get in these situations? I should get a job at the library'.

I went back to the front door about ten minutes later, and it looked like something from an abattoir! There was blood all over the place, the three doormen (registered and unregistered) were laughing amongst each other and chatting as best of friends, clothes ripped, faces bloodied and bruised. I asked them if everything was okay. They replied, "Yeah," and suggested they had better stay on the door together for the rest of the night. I agreed. I don't think any of them remembered me being there just before the fight or what they were actually fighting for. I wasn't bothered; job done, as far as I was concerned. Funny how a war can bring men together.

Nobody seriously injured, (registered or unregistered).

No ongoing wars (registered or unregistered).

No egos were damaged (registered or unregistered).

The alpha males were friends (registered and unregistered).

48.

Wrong Place at the Wrong Time

One night on the door, I had an invitation back for a cup of coffee with one of my doormen, or should I say doorperson. She was a woman I was employing at the time. She was a bodybuilder, pretty and was not scared or fazed by the reputation of anybody. She was a good asset for us working this particular venue as it was always kicking off and women were just as handy with their fists and glasses as the men. To be honest, they always were, but when it came to asking them to leave a venue, they always turned into a lady and played the gender card, that a man should not touch them, while supping on their pint and smoking their roll-up and showing their tattooed arms. So, having 'Mona The Barbarian' on the door was a great help and, like I say, she could handle the men kicking off too.

So, that night, we finished our shift and we left the venue in separate cars and I followed her to her place to get my cup of coffee and, if I was lucky, a protein bar to dip in my cup of coffee; can't imagine her having custard creams. So, we got back to Mona's house, we went inside and she went into the kitchen and put the kettle on. She invited me to take a seat at her kitchen table while she went to get changed out of her doorperson outfit, black jacket, black trousers and white shirt. While Mona was away upstairs getting changed, I was looking around her dining room, admiring her bodybuilding trophies and bodybuilding pictures and tubs of protein and tubs of creatine, fitness magazines and some kind of workout charts. I started to crave a bag of crisps; must have been the rebel in me.

Mona entered the dining room wearing shorts and a vest carrying two half-cups of coffee. I was looking at her big solid shoulders, big solid arms, big solid legs, big solid chest, thinking this is going to be embarrassing if, after the warm half-cup of coffee is finished, she decides she wants a workout. I was a martial artist and ex-boxer and played football on a Saturday and a Sunday. I wasn't really into bodybuilding. My chosen sports were all about keeping your body slim. I had visions of me getting thrown all over the place, being put into some kind of chokehold and not being strong enough to wrestle myself free. Mona took control of the conversation, all about working out, dieting, bodybuilding competitions, all the bodybuilding stars she had met. She explained what all her trophies were for, what her pictures were about; she was talking that much about all this I could feel my ears might need a shot of steroids to cope.

I was bored and trying to think of an excuse to leave when the loud knocking on the door started. I looked at Mona and continued to ask her who it was knocking on her door at 3 in the morning. She told me it was probably her ex, a bodybuilding doorman, and that he was stalking her. She told me not to worry about it - she would go and deal with the situation. I could tell she was angry as her veins were pumping and her muscles seemed to grow. I was wondering if she was going to turn green - just my luck I end up with a cross between the Hulk and Princess Fiona dragging me all over the place! The knocking started getting louder and Mona's boyfriend began shouting abuse. Mona started shouting back at him. She opened the door and they were both just screaming abuse at each other. I started scanning the kitchen for something I could use as a weapon if her boyfriend started flexing his muscles with me, then I heard the noise I've heard 1000 times before; the noise of scuffling and fighting. I walked to the dining room door just to have a sneaky look at what was going on, to be a gent and go to the aid of the woman in need. The noise of screaming and shouting was really loud now. I knew that the neighbours would be awake and somebody would have rung the police to attend. I took a sneaky look from the dining room into the hallway; there was a mass of muscle on the floor with Mona on top. Mona had her arms in a chokehold around the neck of some BIG bodybuilder. I could see his face was red and he was choking out; it's what I have seen used before by doormen called a 'sleeper'. I never did them; we learnt about them in Martial Arts, but not for me. My best sleeper was a left hook! I knew she was trying to put him to sleep; his head went limp and I could see he had passed out. Mona looked up at me, gave me a smile and a wink and told me I had better get myself off. As she was saying this, blue lights appeared outside her house. The police had arrived. I just knew it! Whatever happened now, I was going to be involved once again in something that didn't concern me and I was going to have to explain to her indoors why I ended up in a house where there was a version of wrestle mania happening. A police van and a police car pulled up as I started to make a quick getaway.

"Stop there," was shouted at me. I suppose that's better than freeze.

"Where do you think you're going? What's been happening here? Alright, Matty?" They knew me.

"Nothing to do with me; I was just having a cup of coffee, picking up some bodybuilding routines" I replied as I lifted my arm up and flexed my bicep.

I heard a policewoman shout, "We better get an ambulance, I think he's dead."

I rolled my eyes and knew nobody was dead and, as usual, they were over-reacting.

"No, forget it, it's okay, he's alive and breathing."

Yeah, no shit, Mrs Sherlock, somebody breathing gives it away that they're alive. I heard a commotion and noise, the one I have heard about 1001 times before, the noise of scuffling and fighting. It was Mona resisting arrest. I looked up and could see her in the doorway of her house, struggling with police, or should I say, the police were struggling with her, then the bodybuilder boyfriend appeared, looking like he was drunk. He started to get involved and started pulling at the police to get off his girlfriend, screaming at the police not to arrest Mona. The policeman who had stopped me got on his radio and called for back-up. He turned to me and told me not to move and ran towards where the scuffle was going on. Not a chance I was staying there! The neighbours in their pyjamas were out on the street watching the commotion, and there were neighbours leaning out of upstairs windows with mobile phones, probably recording all the events.

A few hours later, I was playing (trying to) Sunday morning football, when a police car pulls up to our football pitch. nothing unusual there - the team was full of rogues. They shouted me over and placed me in handcuffs and told me that

I was under arrest. I shouted to the lads to get my car keys out of my pocket and take my car home along with my clothes.

It turned out that after the police managed to arrest the Hulk and Hulkess, they searched the house and found steroids, a few cannabis plants, some cocaine, and all sorts of other medicinal aids, and because I had been seen leaving there, as usual, the police had put two and two together and come up with 7 and a half.

I was put in the cells then let out to be questioned, then put back in the cells, then let out to be questioned, then released on bail. When I got home, I told the wife I had missed my Sunday dinner and had been arrested because the football was that bad. Of course, she didn't believe me, but she just never bothered to ask as long as I paid the bills, and she got a few holidays a year.

The following weekend on the door, Mona turned up and apologised for what happened. She told me she'd started to resist arrest because the police didn't believe It was her who put her boyfriend to sleep and thought it was me. She couldn't control her anger at being disrespected, so kicked off. She told them I had nothing to do with anything going on at that house, and that no charges would probably come to me, because I was innocent. Yeah, no shit, Mrs Hulklock! Mona apologised again and then said,

"You fancy coming back to mine after work for a coffee?"

49.

Cookie Drugs

One night on the door, I was working this real nice venue. I loved it; easy money, nice clientele, never any trouble; a few issues to deal with now and then, but easy money - just the way I like it. One of the old-school doormen came in. He'd been retired a while, but could look after himself. He used to turn up at my boxing gym now and then to do some training. He was agile, strong and could bang a good combination out; well-respected round my area. He used to work at clubs, pubs and bars; he was working a rave club just before I started working the door and he was very anti-drugs.

We started chatting to each other while I was working the door, supping on a cup of black coffee. I was looking at him thinking he wasn't quite right. He looked like he'd taken an ecstasy tablet or two. He'd got a semi gun on and was just not being himself. I thought to myself, 'I'll just ask him', even though I already knew the reply he was going to give me, so I asked him as quietly as I could, bearing in mind I was working a venue playing music, full of people trying to talk above the music and with it being on a main road, traffic constantly passing.

"Hey, mate. I don't mean to be out of order here, but have you taken some pills?"

He rolled his eyes and replied, "Yeah, that's what I'm into now."

I was shocked! He used to be so anti-drugs.

"Can you do me a favour?" he asked me. "I live just outside of town now, in the sticks, I'm in with a right crowd of high society, money people, barristers, solicitors, business people, high-ranking police officers, the Full Monty."

I was listening, thinking, 'What kind of favour can I do for him that will concern the likes of that sort of people?' Not my cup of tea; I'm just a working-class lad off a council estate. Sometimes I was known locally and friends from the other parts of town would sing a song about me: 'HE'S JUST A FAT NUNNY GYPO'.

He continued to tell me that once a month, the area he lived in all liked to meet up at and do wife-swapping and have orgies and all that carry on, car keys chucked in the fishbowl. I had a giggle to myself; I'd never been to one of these parties, not for me all that, but I thought if I did go to one of these parties, I'd put my hand in the fishbowl and end up pulling out a fish rather than a set of car keys!

He continued to tell me that they all liked to get out their heads on cocaine and ecstasy tablets just to help them relax, but that the person who used to supply these parties had gone. He never elaborated any more about this person to me, just told me he had gone. Then, he asked me if I could sort him out or did I know anybody who would be discrete and supply him to supply these parties they had. It would only be once a month.

I had a think, then told him, "Not sure, mate, I'm like how you used to be, I'm not into drugs, or the supply of drugs. Big risk here if the Old Bill are involved. Anything goes wrong, and if I've put you on to somebody, I would be in deep shit as well just for introducing you to a supplier."

He turned his head around, left and then right, just to make sure nobody was listening, then quietly said,

"No, honestly, it will go no further than me who I get the gear off, and I don't know the going rate for these drugs, but they pay over the odds for discretion."

As he finished saying that, the sound of 'JACKPOT' started ringing in my ears!

"Okay, when do you want your gear? How much? I'll ask around for you, see what I can do."

He smiled, we exchanged phone numbers and he told me he'd be in touch.

A few days later, I received a sort of coded text message from my old doorman friend. Coded my arse! Stevie Wonder could have read the text message and sussed it out; that's why I don't get involved in all that malarkey - drugs are for mugs. The text message had information telling me what they required for the High Society orgy. I wasn't interested in any of it so thought, 'Fuck it, I'll just give him a reply with a stupid price on it, put some mark-up on it for myself'. I didn't see it as dealing, I saw it as being in the know, and knowing somebody who would knowingly give something to somebody who knew not to ask questions, if you know what I mean. And if he didn't want to pay the price I had given him, that would be fine with me because I didn't want to be involved in all this sordid sort of carry on anyway, especially when police and legal people were involved. Fuck that; I could go missing.

A few hours later and I received another coded text message from my old doorman friend. I was beginning to feel a bit like that well-known government agent, Johnny English! It basically agreed to the price, and asked when it could be picked up. So, I made arrangements and this was how it used to work.

The venue I worked at had flats above it and the entrance to the flats was beside the main door where we worked. I had a very good close friend who lived in one of these flats and he let me have the key to the front entrance to the flats. As you went through the front door of the main entrance, there was a long corridor leading to a stairway. On the left-hand side of the corridor was a small cupboard which contained an electrical meter linked to each flat. I used to work the venue on my own on a Sunday night, so as I was stood on the door right next to the entrance to the flats. I would make sure the door was unlocked, somebody would turn up at approximately 8 pm, place a takeaway in the small cupboard, and be gone straight away. At 8.15 pm, my old doorman friend would turn up, go and visit the cupboard and pick up the takeaway he'd ordered. Then, at 8.30 pm, somebody would turn up to collect the payment for the takeaway. Easy; nothing to do with me and neither party had to know who they were dealing with unless they decided to hide out and watch from a distance. This went on for quite a while, then, as usual, something went wrong. One time, the old doorman friend of mine didn't turn up, so the delivery man started to get irate and take it out on me. I managed to calm him down with a bit of my Wado Ryu (Peace and Harmony), and told him I would sort it. I messaged my friend and got no reply until the next morning when he told me he had to leave the country urgently. He asked me if I could drop off the takeaway on the Saturday night as he didn't think he would be back. I told him no chance; I was working the door. One hour later, he rang me and told me he had spoken to some of the High Society Orgy Party members and they would pay me my doorman wages for the night and a bonus, plus the price of the takeaway to deliver. I told him I would drop off the takeaway at 7 pm on Saturday night, then be gone really quick. I didn't start work on the door until 8, so I had the idea to charge them for missing my door work but still going in to work anyway. Everything was agreed.

On Saturday afternoon, I received a phone call from my friend. He told me to write down this address, gave me a set of directions over the phone and told me I was expected at 7 pm. That night, I set off to the High Society Orgy address. It took me a while but I eventually found the house, or should I say mansion. It was outside a small village. The mansion could not fully be seen from the road due to tall trees, high walls and big electronic gates; just what I'd expected. I got out of my car and pressed the buzzer on the intercom,

"Hello, I'm a friend of (says retired doorman name). I have a takeaway here for you."

"Okay, come on in," came the reply back through the telecom system. The voice sounded like a Dalek out of Dr Who.

The gates swung open and I drove down the drive. I was very nervous, on the border of being scared. My mind was all over the place - what if they kidnapped me and fed me to a gimp? What if they chucked my car keys in the middle and I ended up with a Margaret Thatcher lookalike? What if there is police there and it was a setup? What if Jeremy Beadle appears? In my rear-view mirror, I could see the big electric gates closing behind me. It was too late to reverse my car out of the driveway. As I pulled up outside the main entrance, a tall dignified old man was there to greet me. I stopped my car and passed him his takeaway, then he passed me a payment for his takeaway, smiled at me and then said,

"You have a cheeky face; have we met before? You sure you can't come in for a quick drink? My friends would love to meet you!"

"No, thank you very much, I have to get home to feed my goldfish."

"Oh, I'm pretty sure your goldfish will not mind if you stay for a quick drink or two." He was fucking trying to groom me, I knew he was. He had Margaret Thatcher in that mansion waiting for me in stockings and suspenders! Well, there was no way he was getting me out of my car and into the mansion.

"No, honestly, you wouldn't want to see my goldfish upset. Bye," I shouted as I started to drive off. I caught a quick look at some of the people there as I drove past a big bay window. Some of them raised their wine glasses to me in a 'cheers' motion.

All the way driving back into town, I was wondering what would have happened if I had taken up the offer of a drink. I was wondering if they believed I had an irate hungry goldfish at home.

Six months later, I was up in court for some minor charge. The magistrate, who I believed had a soft spot for goldfish, and the prosecuting solicitor for the CPS, who was stood in the bay window, for some reason threw my charges out of court due to some legal technicality. Funny who you bump into when you least expect it.

I wonder if it had anything to do with my cheeky face?